METTĀ
Loving-kindness in Buddhism

Sujin Boriharnwanaket
Translated by Nina van Gorkom

April 2024

Published in April 2024 by:
Zolag
www.zolag.co.uk

ISBN 9781897633526

Translated by Nina van Gorkom

Contents

1 Introduction 1

2 Conditions and impediments 11

3 Overcoming anger 25

4 Mettā in daily life 35

5 Characteristic of mettā 47

6 Mettā in action and speech 61

7 Benefits of mettā 73

8 The blessings of mettā 81

9 Cause and result in life 91

10 Mettā: foundation of the world 101

11 Selected texts 109

12 Pāli glossary 123

13 Books by Nina van Gorkom 139

Editors note

The Pāli glossary is generic and not specifically made for this book. Although there are Pāli words in the text that may not be in this glossary, they are defined as they are introduced.

1
Introduction

Ajahn Sujin Boriharnwanaket's approach to the development of loving-kindness–mettā–is very direct. She aims at the practical application of the Buddha's teachings in daily life. The Buddha teaches the way to eradicate what is unwholesome and to develop what is wholesome. Mettā is an essential way of wholesomeness. However, it is difficult to develop it because we usually think of ourselves. The development of mettā is most beneficial both to ourselves and others: it will lead to less selfishness and it is of vital importance to harmony and peace in society.

This book is a compilation of a series of lectures by Ajahn Sujin held at the Bovornives Temple in Bangkok. During her lectures, questions were brought up and therefore part of this book contains questions and answers. Ajahn Sujin explains that in order to develop mettā we have to know exactly what it is and when it arises. We are likely to confuse selfish affection with mettā and then mettā cannot be developed. Ajahn Sujin quotes from the Buddhist scriptures, the "Tipiṭaka", and from commentaries in order to illustrate the development of mettā as taught by the Buddha. She always stresses that the development should conform to the teachings of the Buddha as they have come to us at present. Formerly people were used to accepting what their teachers said without going themselves to the source of the teachings, the Tipiṭaka. Ajahn Sujin has always greatly encouraged people to read the scriptures themselves, to consider them and to prove the truth to themselves through the practical application of the Dhamma, the Buddha's teachings, in daily life.

When she started her lectures more than twenty-five years ago, there were hardly any Thai translations of the commentaries to the Tipiṭaka. Each time she needed the commentary to the suttas she was going to quote during her next lecture, she asked one of the monks for a translation from Pāli into Thai of the corresponding parts of the commentaries. It was also due to her encouragement that the interest in the teachings and commentaries of both monks and lay people grew and more commentaries were translated into Thai. At present, the Tipiṭaka has been reprinted in Thailand in such a way that each sutta or each section is immediately followed by the corresponding commentary which gives the explanation of that text. Ajahn Sujin helps people not only to investigate the sources of the teachings but also to have right understanding of the application of the teachings, in daily life. Her lectures can be heard on the radio, morning and evening. The radio stations which send out her lectures are in different parts of Thailand and their number increases. Her lectures can also be heard in neighbouring countries, such as Laos, Malaysia and Cambodia.

With my deepest appreciation of Ajahn Sujin's guidance and support and with great pleasure I offer the translation of this book on mettā to the English-speaking readers. I made a free translation adapted to "Western people" with some changes, additions and footnotes. The Thais are familiar with Pāli terms and their meanings, but these are difficult to understand for those who begin to study the Buddhist teachings. In order to help the reader to understand this book I will now explain a few notions in this book which are essential for understanding mettā and for its application in daily life.

Mettā cannot be developed if people do not know their own "mental states" in Pāli, cittas. What we take for "my mind" are actually many different moments of consciousness, cittas, which change all the time. There is only one citta at a time which arises and then falls away immediately, to be succeeded by the next citta. Our life is an unbroken series of cittas arising in succession. Each citta experiences an object. Seeing is a citta which experiences colour through the eye-sense. Hearing is a citta which experiences sound through the ear-sense. Cittas experience objects through the six doorways of eyes, ears, nose, tongue, body-sense and mind.

Cittas are variegated: some cittas are wholesome, kusala cittas; some are unwholesome, akusala cittas; some are neither kusala nor akusala. When there is mettā with the citta, the citta is kusala, but when there is selfish affection or anger with the citta, the citta is akusala. There is one citta at a time, but each citta is accompanied by several mental factors–cetasikas–which each perform their own function while they accompany the citta. Some cetasikas, such as feeling and remembrance, accompany each citta, while other types of cetasikas can accompany only akusala cittas or only kusala cittas. Akusala cittas are accompanied by unwholesome mental factors, such as attachment, lobha, or aversion, dosa; and kusala cittas are accompanied by "beautiful mental factors" such as generosity or mettā.

Cittas and cetasikas are realities which arise because of their appropriate conditions. For example, wholesome qualities and defilements which arose in the past can condition the arising of such qualities at present. Cittas arise and then fall away, but since each citta is succeeded by the following one, wholesome qualities and defilements can be accumulated from moment to moment, and thus there are conditions for their arising at the present time.

Seeing, hearing, smelling, tasting and the experience of bodily impressions are cittas which are neither kusala nor akusala, they are cittas which are results of kamma, vipāka cittas. Unwholesome deeds and wholesome deeds done in the past can bring about pleasant and unpleasant results at present. Kamma is actually intention or volition. The unwholesome or wholesome volition which motivates a deed is accumulated from moment to moment and thus it can produce result later on. Kamma produces result in the form of rebirth-consciousness or, in the course of life, in the form of seeing, hearing and the other sense impressions. Seeing, hearing and the other sense impressions experience pleasant and unpleasant objects, depending on the kamma which produces these vipākacittas. When a pleasant object is seen, attachment is likely to arise after the seeing, and when an unpleasant object is seen, aversion is likely to arise after the seeing. The sense impressions are followed by akusala cittas more often than by kusala cittas. There is no self who can direct or control the cittas which arise, they arise because of their own conditions, they are non-self, anattā. Right understanding of the different cittas which arise is the factor which can condition the development of more wholesome qualities.

The Buddha taught that what we take for "our mind" and "our body" are ever-changing phenomena which arise and then fall away immediately, they are impermanent and anattā. Citta and cetasika, consciousness and mental factors are mental phenomena: in Pāli, nāma. Physical phenomena are called, in Pāli, rūpa. Nāma and rūpa are ultimate realities or absolute realities. Nāmas such as seeing, mettā or anger, and rūpas such as colour, sound or hardness, are ultimate realities. They each have their own characteristic which can be directly experienced when it appears. They are real for everybody. Their names can be changed, but their characteristics cannot be changed. There is ultimate truth and there is conventional truth. Without the study of the Buddha's teachings one knows only conventional truth: the world of person, being, self, trees and cars. These are concepts we can think of, but they are not ultimate realities which can be directly experienced. Conventional truth is not denied in Buddhism, but the difference between ultimate truth and conventional truth is pointed out so that they can be distinguished from each other. Even when we have understood that what we take for a person consists of nāma and rūpa which arise and fall away, we can still think of persons. We can think of them in the unwholesome way: with selfish affection or with anger, or in the wholesome way: with mettā or with compassion.

Buddhism teaches different ways of wholesomeness: dāna or generosity, sīla or good moral conduct and bhāvanā or mental development, which includes the development of tranquillity, samatha, and the development of insight, vipassanā. There are different types of kusala cittas. Sometimes they are accompanied by right understanding, paññā, and sometimes they are not accompanied by right understanding. Dāna and sīla can be performed also without right understanding, but for mental development paññā is necessary. There are different levels of paññā. When kusala citta with generosity arises it can be accompanied by paññā which knows that generosity is kusala and which knows that a wholesome action will produce a pleasant result. That is one level of paññā. There is paññā at the level of intellectual understanding of the Buddhist teachings, understanding that the nāmas and rūpas which arise because of conditions are impermanent and anattā. Paññā in samatha, tranquil meditation, is of a different level again. It is not merely theoretical understanding, it realises precisely when the citta is kusala and when it is akusala; it sees the disadvantages of akusala and the benefits of kusala. Paññā in samatha knows the right conditions to develop calm by means of a meditation subject. Calm accompanies kusala citta and when its characteristic is known through direct experience it can be developed. It is developed by concentrating on one of the meditation subjects; but if one just tries to concentrate on one object without right understanding, calm cannot be developed. There are particular meditation subjects of samatha, as explained in the Path of Purification (Visuddhimagga), which is an Encyclopedia on Buddhism, written by the commentator Buddhaghosa. Mettā is among the meditation subjects of samatha. When calm has been developed there can be the attainment of jhāna, absorption. At the moment of jhāna there are no sense impressions and one is free from defilements which are bound up with them. The jhānacitta is of a higher plane of consciousness. However, after the jhānacittas have fallen away defilements can arise again. Through samatha, defilements are temporarily subdued but they are not eradicated. It is extremely difficult to attain jhāna and only very few people are able to do it. Those who can attain jhāna with mettā as a meditation subject, can with a mind full of mettā pervade the whole world and all beings. This is the "extension of mettā to all beings", as referred to in this book. As Ajahn Sujin explains, also those who do not intend to develop a high degree of calm can and should develop mettā in daily life. If they know precisely when the citta is kusala and when akusala and if they know the characteristic of mettā, they can develop it, and at such moments there is calm with the citta.

The development of insight or vipassanā is different from the development of samatha. The method and aim of these two ways of mental development are different. The development of insight is the development of the right understanding of ultimate realities, of nāma and rūpa, in order to eradicate the wrong view of self. Through insight, all defilements and latent tendencies of defilements can eventually be completely eradicated. In the development of insight one does not try to concentrate on one object, but through mindfulness or awareness, sati, right understanding of any reality which appears through one of the six doors is developed. Right understanding of realities can be developed at any place and any time, in daily life; one does not have to go to a quiet place. Sati is a wholesome cetasika which is non-forgetful, aware of the nāma or rūpa which appears at the present moment. At the very moment of sati, direct understanding of the reality which appears can be developed, so that realities can eventually be seen as anattā. Satipaṭṭhāna, the application of mindfulness, is another term for the development of right understanding of nāma and rūpa. In the beginning sati and paññā are weak, but each moment they arise they develop, even when this is not noticeable. They can develop from moment to moment, from life to life.

The reader will come across the term sati-sampajañña, which stands for sati and paññā. Sampajaññā is another word for paññā. Sati and paññā are different cetasikas which each perform their own function, but both of them are needed in order to develop an understanding of the reality appearing at the present moment. If there is only awareness of realities without any understanding, the goal, seeing realities as they are, cannot be reached. Sati-sampajañña is anattā, it cannot be induced. There can only be sati-sampajañña when there are the right conditions. These conditions are: listening to the Dhamma as it is explained by someone with right understanding, and careful consideration of the Dhamma. First there has to be theoretical understanding of nāma and rūpa. One has to know that nāma is the reality which experiences something, and that rūpa is the reality which does not know anything. One has to understand that seeing is nāma which experiences what appears through the eyes, visible object, and that visible object is rūpa. It is necessary to understand that seeing is different from thinking of people which can arise after seeing, to understand that different nāmas experience objects through six doors. We may believe that we can touch our body, but in reality it consists of different elements which appear one at a time. Through touch hardness or heat can be experienced, not a body. The body is a concept which is made up by thinking, not an ultimate reality. When one has understood what ultimate realities are, different from conventional truth, there can be conditions for the arising of sati, of mindfulness. Sati is directly aware and attentive to the nāma or rūpa which presents itself right now. We experience time and again rūpas through the body-sense, such as hardness or softness, but there is forgetfulness and ignorance of these realities. We usually pay attention to a thing or the body which is hard or soft, to the concept of a "whole". When sati arises it can be aware of a rūpa such as hardness or softness, or of a nāma which experiences these rūpas, and at that moment these realities can be investigated by paññā. They can be known as rūpa or nāma, which arise because of their own conditions, and which are anattā. Paññā is developed in different stages of insight. First, the difference between nāma and rūpa has to be realised, otherwise there cannot be the direct understanding of the arising and falling away of nāma and rūpa, which is a higher stage of insight. It can be understood in theory that nāma is different from rūpa, but when they actually present themselves the difference between their characteristics is not directly known. We tend to confuse realities such as hearing and sound or seeing and visible object. Sati can only be aware of one reality at a time; and only if there is awareness over and over again can paññā can develop so that nāma and rūpa can be seen as they are.

When paññā has been fully developed there can be the attainment of enlightenment: the experience of nibbāna, the unconditioned reality. Citta, cetasika and rūpa are ultimate realities which arise because of conditions and then fall away. Nibbāna is not rūpa, it is not a place where one can go; it is nāma. Nibbāna is the ultimate reality which is an unconditioned nāma, it does not arise and fall away. Nibbāna is called the end of suffering, dukkha, the end of the unsatisfactoriness inherent in all conditioned realities which arise and fall away. There are four stages of enlightenment and, at each stage, defilements are subsequently eradicated, until they are all eradicated at the final stage, the stage of the arahat–the perfected one.

The objects of satipaṭṭhāna, of the development of right understanding, are ultimate realities, nāma and rūpa. Mettā is directed towards beings, it has beings or persons as objects. Beings are not ultimate realities, they are conventional truths. However, it is most beneficial to develop both satipaṭṭhāna and mettā, as Ajahn Sujin explains. When there is awareness of nāma and rūpa there can still be thinking of beings, thinking is a type of nāma which arises because of conditions. We usually think of people with akusala cittas, cittas with attachment or aversion. Instead of thinking with akusala cittas we can learn to think with mettā-citta. Mettā-citta is a type of nāma and if there can be awareness of it we will see it as a conditioned reality, non-self. If we do not cling to a concept of "my mettā", mettā will be purer.

Ajahn Sujin emphasises that the development of satipaṭṭhāna conditions the arising of mettā more often. When satipaṭṭhāna is developed, defilements such as conceit, avarice and jealousy, which are impediments to mettā, will eventually be eradicated. The understanding that both we ourselves and other people are only citta, cetasika and rūpa, will condition more mettā. If we understand that our akusala cittas arise because of conditions, we will also understand that the akusala cittas of someone else are conditioned. We will be less inclined to judge others and we will have more understanding of their problems. We can learn to become, as Ajahn Sujin says, "an understanding person", someone who sympathises and helps others. If they do not respond to our kindness we can still treat them as friends. True friendship does not depend on the attitude of someone else, it arises with the mettā-citta.

Mettā is one of the "perfections"- excellent qualities the Buddha developed during countless previous lives when he was a Bodhisatta, a being destined for Buddhahood. People who have confidence in the Buddha's teachings and develop satipaṭṭhāna can develop the perfections together with mindfulness of nāma and rūpa. The perfections, and thus also mettā, are necessary conditions for the attainment of enlightenment. The aim of the development of the perfections is the elimination of defilements.

Ajahn Sujin helps people to know their own citta, to know when it is kusala citta and when akusala citta. When they have right understanding of their cittas, they will not delude themselves and take for mettā what is akusala. Ajahn Sujin's explanation on mettā is essential for the understanding of what mettā is, and of the way how it can be developed. Her explanations are very convincing and direct and can be of great assistance to practise mettā in daily life. The many texts she quotes from the Buddhist scriptures can be a reminder and encouragement to practise mettā in daily life.

The quotations in this book are taken from the Tipiṭaka and from some of the commentaries, including the Atthasālinī (Expositor), the commentary to the first book of the Abhidhamma (Dhammasangaṇi), and the Path of Purification (Visuddhimagga). The English translations of these texts are available at the Pāli Text Society: https://palitextsociety.org/

I want to retain the Pāli terms in this book because it is useful to learn some of them. The English equivalents are often unsatisfactory since these stem from Western philosophy and therefore give an association of meaning different from the meaning they have in the Buddhist teachings. I wish to acknowledge my appreciation to the "Dhamma Study and Support Foundation" and to the publisher Alan Weller who made the printing of the translation of this book possible. *Nina van Gorkom*

2

Conditions and impediments

Mettā, loving-kindness, can be cultivated when we know its characteristic. When there is true mettā other people are considered as friends: there is a feeling of closeness and sympathy, we have tender care for them and we want to do everything for their benefit and happiness. At such moments the citta is gentle, there is no conceit–māna, which is the condition for asserting oneself, for showing one's own importance and for disparaging others.

If there is an earnest wish to develop mettā, we want to eliminate akusala dhammas, also those which we usually do not notice. We do not realise the extent of our conceit, jealousy, stinginess, aversion and other defilements. When we develop mettā we will begin to notice many kinds of defilements, and as mettā is accumulated more there will be less opportunity for the arising of unwholesomeness.

Conceit is a defilement which impedes mettā. When there is mettā, we think of the well-being of someone else, whereas when there is conceit, we find ourselves important. If we wish to eliminate conceit and to develop mettā we must know the characteristic of conceit. We read in the Atthasālinī (Expositor, Book II, Part II, Chapter 2, 372) about conceit:

> "Conceit", "overweening" and "conceitedness" signify mode and state. "Loftiness" is in the sense of rising upwards or of springing over others. "Haughtiness", i.e. in whom conceit arises, him it lifts up, keeps upraised. "Flaunting a flag" is in the sense of swelling above others. "Assumption" means uplifting; conceit favours the mind all round. Of many flags the flag which rises above others is called a banner. So conceit arising repeatedly in the sense of excelling with reference to subsequent conceits is like a banner. That mind which desires the banner is said to be desirous of the banner (i.e., self advertisement). Such a state is desire for self-advertisement. And that is of the citta, not of a real self; hence "desire of the citta for self-advertisement". Indeed, the citta associated with conceit wants a banner, and its state is reckoned as banner-conceit.

When we learn about the characteristic of conceit we can see the difference between the moment of akusala citta and of mettā. Akusala citta does not have the characteristic of gentleness and tenderness, at such a moment there is no feeling of closeness and friendship for others. If we want to develop mettā there must be "sati-sampajañña", mindfulness and understanding, in order to know when there is kuṣala citta and when there is akusala citta. At the moment of conceit there cannot be mettā.

Jealousy is another defilement which is an impediment to mettā. When we are jealous of someone we certainly do not treat him as a friend. If we really want to develop mettā in our daily life, we should be aware of its characteristic of sympathy and tenderness and we should realise that mettā cannot go together with jealousy.

The Atthasālinī (Book II, Part II, Chapter 2, 373) states about envy:

> In the exposition of envy, "envy at the gains, honour, reverence, affection, salutation, worship accruing to others" is that envy which has the characteristic of not enduring, or of grumbling at the prosperity of others, saying concerning others' gains, etc., "What is the use to these people of all this?"

The person who has attained the first stage of enlightenment, the sotāpanna, has completely eradicated jealousy because he sees the characteristics of realities as they are: mental phenomena (nāma dhammas) and physical phenomena (rūpa dhammas), arising because of their appropriate conditions. He realises that there isn't anybody who can create gains for himself, or who can cause others to honour him, to greet him or to pay respect to him. In fact, obtaining gains and receiving honour and respect from others depends on conditions. Therefore, there should not be jealousy. When there is jealousy there is no mettā. All dhammas, realities, are anattā (non-self), kusala dhammas as well as akusala dhammas; they arise because of their appropriate conditions. So long as one is not yet an "ariyan", a person who has attained enlightenment, there are conditions for jealousy. One is not only jealous of those who are not one's relatives or friends but even of those who are near and dear to oneself.

Stinginess is another defilement which is an impediment to mettā. The Atthasālinī (in the same section, 373) states that there is stinginess as to five things:

> dwelling (the place where one stays)

> family (for a monk this can be the family of servitors to a monastery or relatives)
>
> gain (for a monk: the acquirement of the four requisites)
>
> beauty and praise (one does not want others to be praised because of beauty or merits)
>
> dhamma (one does not want to share knowledge of dhamma)

We read further on (375, 376):

> "Stinginess" is the expression of meanness. "Avariciousness" is the act or mode of being mean. The citta which is mean is the state of one endowed with stinginess. "Let it be for me only and not for another!"–thus wishing not to diffuse all one's own acquisitions... The state of such a person is "avarice", a synonym for soft meanness. An ignoble person is churlish. His state is "ignobleness", a name for hard stinginess. Verily, a person endowed with it hinders another from giving to others. And this also has been said (Kindred Sayings, I, 120):
>
> Malicious, miserly, ignoble, wrong...
>
> Such men hinder the feeding of the poor...
>
> "niggardly" person seeing mendicants causes his mind to shrink as by sourness. His state is "niggardliness". Another way:–"niggardliness" is a "spoon-feeding".
>
> For when the pot is full to the brim, one takes food from it by a spoon with the edge bent on all sides; it is not possible to get a spoonful; so is the citta of a mean person bent in. When it is bent in, the body also is bent in, recedes, is not diffused –thus stinginess is said to be niggardliness.

> "Lack of generosity of citta" is the state of a mind which is shut and gripped, so that it is not stretched out in the mode of making gifts, etc. in doing service to others. But because the mean person wishes not to give to others what belongs to himself, and only wishes to receive what belongs to others, therefore this meanness should be understood to have the characteristic of hiding or seizing one's own property, occurring thus:
> "May it be for me and not for another!"

The commentator investigates here the citta of the ordinary person who has not yet eradicated avarice. Only the ariyan has eradicated avarice completely. When aversion, conceit, jealousy or stinginess arise, there is no mettā with the citta. If we want to develop mettā, we should acquire a refined knowledge of our different cittas. The characteristics of the cittas which think of particular persons should be investigated. Mettā should not be restricted to a particular group of people. We should continue to develop mettā evermore. There can never be enough mettā.

The Buddha showed in many different suttas the benefit of the development of mettā. We read in the Kindred Sayings (I, Sagāthā vagga, Chapter X, The Yakkhas, §4, Maṇibhadda):

> The Exalted One was once staying among the Magadhese, at the Maṇimāla temple, in the haunt of the yakkha Maṇibhadda. Then that yakkha drew near to the Exalted One, and before him uttered the verse:
>
> To one of mind alert luck ever comes;
> He prospers with increasing happiness
> For him tomorrow is a better day.
> And wholly from all hate is he released.
>
> The Buddha said:

> ...For him whose mind ever by night and day
> In harmlessness, in kindness takes delight,
> Bearing his share in love for all that lives,
> In him no hate is found toward anyone.

Thus we see the great benefit of the development of mettā.

Mettā can be developed as a subject of tranquil meditation, samatha. If there is right understanding of the development of calm with this subject, a high degree of calm, even absorption, jhāna, can be attained. The cittas which attain absorption, jhānacittas, are of a higher plane of citta. At the moments of jhānacitta there are no sense impressions and one is temporarily free from defilements. However, after the jhānacittas have fallen away, defilements arise again. The development of tranquillity with mettā as meditation subject will not lead to the eradication of anger, dosa. Only the development of satipaṭṭhāna, right understanding of realities, leads to the eradication of defilements. Defilements are eradicated subsequently at four stages of enlightenment. Only at the fourth stage, the stage of the arahat, all defilements are eradicated. At the third stage, the stage of the "non-returner", anāgāmī, anger or aversion is eradicated. The anāgāmī has no more anger and is full of mettā.

The development of right understanding of realities, satipaṭṭhāna, can be the condition for more mettā. Paññā, right understanding, knows that what one takes for beings, people or self are only mental phenomena, nāma dhammas, and physical phenomena, rūpa dhammas. We use conventional terms and names for the different beings and things which appear, but in reality there are only nāmas and rūpas which arise because of conditions and then fall away. Each citta which falls away is succeeded by the next one, and also rūpas which fall away are replaced so long as there are conditions for them to be produced.

Someone said that while he is not engaged in any activity he finds that he is distracted, that he has akusala cittas. He wishes, in order to have kusala cittas, to recite stanzas about mettā for a long time. If one develops satipaṭṭhāna however, one should remember that even feeling distracted or dull can be the object of awareness. In such circumstances, sati can be aware immediately of the characteristic which appears and then there are kusala cittas. It is not easy to know the characteristic of the reality which appears; paññā should really be developed so that there can be precise knowledge of the different characteristics of nāma and rūpa. There must be awareness of the characteristic of the reality which experiences, nāma dhamma, and of the characteristic of the reality which does not know anything, rūpa dhamma. The difference between the characteristics of nāma and rūpa should be clearly distinguished. When there is awareness of the realities which appear one at a time through the doorways of the senses and the mind, through the six doors, their characteristics must be carefully considered and investigated. In that way nāma and rūpa can be understood as they are: as non-self.

The person who believes that he should just recite texts about mettā may not be sure whether there are at such moments kusala cittas or akusala cittas. He may not know that awareness, sati, is necessary for the development of paññā, understanding, which clearly knows the reality appearing at the present moment. Perhaps he may not even know to which purpose he recites texts. If we really want to cultivate mettā we should see the disadvantage of all kinds of akusala, such as aversion, conceit, jealousy and stinginess.

For the development of mettā it is necessary to have a refined, detailed knowledge of one's different cittas. They must be known as they really are. Kusala citta and akusala citta have different characteristics. Even if there is kusala of a slight degree, that moment is completely different from the moments of attachment. If sati and paññā do not arise, one cannot know when there is lobha–attachment–and when there is mettā. If one does not know their different characteristics one may unknowingly develop akusala instead of mettā since one takes for kusala what is in fact akusala. Therefore a precise knowledge of the different characteristics of lobha and mettā is necessary. The Atthasālinī (Book II, Part II, Chapter 2) explains about the many aspects of lobha mentioned in the Dhammasangaṇi. We read about "delight":

> "Delight" refers to this that by greed, beings in any existence feel delight, or greed itself is delighting in. In "passionate delight" we get the first term combined with delight. Craving once arisen to an object is "delight"; arisen repeatedly, it is "passionate delight"...

This is daily life which should really be investigated. When mettā does not arise citta is infatuated by objects, it delights in objects all the time. If there is no awareness we do not know when there is lobha. The clinging to the different objects which are experienced will condition our behaviour, our actions through body and speech, and then we can find out that there is no mettā. When we have learnt through our own experience the characteristic of lobha and of mettā when they arise, we can compare them and clearly know their difference.

We should not only try to develop mettā when anger arises, but also when there is attachment. We should consider with what kind of citta we think of our friends, our circle of relatives, those who are near and dear to us. We should find out whether there are at such moments cittas with mettā or cittas with lobha, and we should learn by our own experience the difference between these moments. If we earnestly wish to develop mettā we should not waste any opportunity to learn about the characteristics of our different cittas so that there are conditions for the development of mettā. It is useless to think that we should develop mettā only when we become angry.

I will now go into some questions with regard to the development of mettā.

Question: The characteristic of lobha is love and attachment. If one says that attachment to relatives and friends is lobha and that it is therefore wrong to be attached to them I think that this does not agree with our ordinary, daily life in the world.

Sujin: If one wants to develop mettā there must be a precise knowledge of one's different cittas. If people only recite texts about mettā it is not sufficient; the characteristic of mettā should be known precisely. When there is mettā there is no anger. However, when we love someone and we are attached to that person there is lobha, not mettā, and lobha can condition anger. We should consider which reality is better, mettā or selfish love, which is actually lobha. When we are in the company of family or friends, there can be mettā and then we can come to know its characteristic. When there is mettā we wish other people's benefit, there is no clinging, no selfish love. True mettā towards someone else cannot condition dislike of that person. Thus, when we have mettā instead of lobha others will benefit from this too. Both the person who has mettā and the person who is the object of mettā will benefit. If there is only lobha in our daily life there are many conditions for dislike and unpleasant feeling. However, to the extent mettā develops there will be less opportunities for the arising of dosa. We will become more considerate and think more often of the benefit of others.

Question: You said that sati and paññā (sati-sampajañña) are necessary for the development of mettā and that one therefore should know the characteristics of sati and paññā. If one does not know them mettā cannot be developed, is that right?

Sujin: There are two kinds of mental development: samatha, tranquil meditation, and vipassanā, the development of insight or right understanding of realities. For both kinds of mental development sati-sampajañña is necessary. However, paññā in samatha is different from paññā in vipassanā. Paññā in samatha knows the way to develop tranquillity, the temporary freedom from defilements. Paññā in the development of vipassanā knows the characteristics of mental phenomena and physical phenomena, of the realities which appear one at a time through the six doors.

Question: Sometimes mettā can arise when one is concerned about other people who are in trouble. At such a moment there is sati but there may not be paññā which knows the characteristic of sati. Is there true mettā at such a moment?

Sujin: When mettā arises the citta is kusala and it is accompanied by sati which is a wholesome reality (sobhana dhamma). One may not have sati-sampajañña so that a higher degree of calm can be developed, but when there is mettā it has to be accompanied by sati, because of conditions. Sati which is nonforgetful of kusala accompanies each kusala citta. Because of accumulations of kusala there can be conditions for different kinds of kusala, for dāna (generosity), for sīla (abstention from unwholesome deeds) or for mettā. Those types of kusala are accompanied by sati but not necessarily by paññā. However, if one wants to develop mettā as subject of calm and attain to higher degrees of calm, sati-sampajañña is necessary. Through sati-sampajañña the difference between the characteristics of mettā and lobha can be known precisely.

Question: I will speak about events in my daily life. Sometimes when I drive the car I recite: "May all beings be happy, may they not suffer any harm or misfortune." When I happened to be in a complicated traffic situation, however, I could at first not be considerate to others. Later on I realised that I did not behave in accordance with the texts about mettā I had recited. I started to consider more those texts and I learnt to apply mettā in the traffic situation. Thus this is the effect of thinking and considering.

Sujin: When you are in a complicated traffic situation do

you think of the words, "May all beings be happy"?

Question: No, I do not think of these words at such moments.

Sujin: The development of mettā is not a matter of thinking of words, but one should know the reality of mettā-citta. Such a moment is different from the moments of annoyance, anger or vengeance.

Question: If I had not recited texts about mettā I would not be considerate in the traffic situation, I would only think of myself.

Sujin: You should have a detailed knowledge of realities, you should find out whether there is at the moment you recite true mettā or just thinking of words. There is true mettā at the moment you are considerate towards others, not when you just recite words.

Question: The reciting does have an effect. If I had not recited I would not have asked myself whether I really wanted other beings to be happy. The fact that I asked myself this was the effect of my recitation.

Sujin: When you asked yourself this, you realised already that mettā is not just reciting words but that it should be in daily life.

Question: Yes, that is true. When I have mettā in the situation I did not recite.

Sujin: Some people only think of reciting texts about mettā, but after they have finished reciting they become angry when something unpleasant occurs. One may recite words about mettā, but mettā may not arise when there are beings or people present. One may recite for a long time, but when something unpleasant happens, where is mettā? How much longer should one then recite so that mettā can arise?

Another questioner: If one thinks that one must recite in order to develop mettā there will not be any result, because one has wrong understanding about the development of mettā. Its development will only be successful if one has mettā in the situation of one's daily life. Since a year or two I have the feeling that I have more mettā than before, and that is only due to Ajahn Sujin's lectures about dhamma I listened to. I always think now of doing things for the benefit and happiness of others, no matter whether it is a small matter or something more important. I feel that when sati arises the citta is gentle. When we abstain from killing mosquitoes or help other beings who are in trouble there is mettā. It happened that at first I did not want to make an effort to help other beings, but later on I could do it, because I considered their benefit and happiness. Sometimes people sell things I do not want to buy, but I still buy them because mettā arises. I do not buy them because I wish to have them or I need them. I think of Ajahn Sujin's words, "It does not matter whether we do a lot or just a little for someone else, but we can consider his benefit and happiness." Whenever I think of these words kusala citta with mettā can arise.

Sujin: Anumodhanā. This is the right understanding of the dhamma, it really is the development of mettā. The Pāli term for development is "bhāvanā" and this literally means: to make become more, to cause to arise often, time and again. Development is not reciting texts with the expectation that as a result a high degree of calm, even absorption, jhānacitta, will arise. There should be mettā in our daily life. We may, when we are alone, recite texts about mettā many times, but when we are in the situation of our daily life mettā may not arise. The real development of mettā is done through our behaviour in the different circumstances of daily life, when we are in the company of other people.

Question: I still think that the reciting of texts on mettā may be beneficial. Reciting is not easy. I may think of people I do not like, such as Mr X. who had done me wrong in the past, but now, while I develop mettā, I think, "May Mr X. be happy, may he not suffer any misfortune". When I recite texts, I do not have to spend any money or make an effort to help someone. I am not ready yet to do these things.

Sujin: The reason is that you did not develop mettā gradually, in daily life. Today you do not see Mr X., but you see other people. Can you find out whether there is mettā now, while you see other people? When one really develops mettā one must know that when there is mettā the citta is free from all that is unwholesome. At such a moment there is no conceit, no idea of making oneself important. Even when we look at other people or think of them, we can do so without looking down on them, without conceit. Mettā can be expressed through the body, even in our gestures, and in our way of speech. No matter with whom we are, sati-sampajañña can arise and we can find out whether the citta at a particular moment is accompanied by mettā or not. We can develop mettā all the time and we should not select the persons towards whom we will have mettā, such as Mr X.

Question: I will start to develop mettā all the time. When I see other people I will think, "May all people be happy, may they not suffer misfortune".

Sujin: Why do you think of all people?

Question: When I look at people I see them as a group.

Sujin: At this moment you know in theory that there are only nāma and rūpa, no beings, people or self. However, you do not know the characteristics of nāma and rūpa. There is no sati-sampajañña which considers each kind of reality which appears. When the characteristics of nāmas and rūpas are clearly known, as they appear one at a time, mettā can be developed more. Thus, there must be sati-sampajañña which knows the characteristic of the citta when there is mettā for such or such person. Otherwise, we could not know whether there is only reciting and thinking of texts about mettā, or sincere mettā for each person we meet.

Question: When I recite texts on mettā there is sometimes no paññā, but there is sati. I wish to extend mettā to all beings.

Sujin: We should know the meaning of "developing mettā"

and of "extending mettā to all beings". If one has not really developed mettā the citta does not wish happiness for anybody one meets. One does not yet have a feeling of friendship for all people, and thus one is not able to extend mettā to all beings. One can begin to develop mettā for other people through body, speech and thoughts, and thus it can gradually increase. When we think of someone else, whoever he may be, or whenever we meet someone else, there can be sincere mettā through body, speech and mind. By the recitation of texts on mettā there will not be any change in the expression of our face or in our speech; mettā will not develop through the recitation of texts. When we meet someone we can consider the citta at that moment, we should know whether we look down on him, even though we do not show this outwardly, but it is just in our mind. Does it happen that we dislike someone's appearance, behaviour or speech? Do we really consider that person as a friend while we speak to him, do we sincerely seek what is beneficial for him and do we want to help him? There is no rule that one should recite particular texts about mettā. If we want to develop mettā we do not have to follow any rule about recitation of texts. We can think of others with kusala citta which is accompanied by mettā: we can think of doing things for his well-being and happiness, of protecting him from misfortune and trouble. When one recites one has to think of words, one has to think whether one should say first "may all beings be happy", or whether one should say first "may all beings be free from suffering". The reality of mettā is not the recitation of texts. Mettā arises when we give help to someone else through actions or through speech, depending on the situation at that moment.

3

Overcoming anger

If we truly know the characteristic of mettā we can develop it. However, we should not think that we can already extend mettā to all beings so that it is boundless. In fact, only people who have developed samatha with mettā as meditation subject and have attained the first stage of jhāna, are able to extend mettā to all beings.

Question: The commentator states that one should recite particular texts about mettā.

Sujin: Does mettā-citta arise according to a particular rule?

Question: No, that is not so.

Sujin: One should know the characteristic of mettā as it is and then one can develop it more and more. However, as I explained, one should not try to extend mettā to all beings straightaway in order to develop it more.

Question: There are forty meditation subjects of samatha and it depends on one's inclination which subject one will develop. Generally one has to recite texts in order to develop meditation subjects, such as the "earth kasina".

Sujin: We should investigate the Tipiṭaka in order to find out whether it is said that we should recite texts. We read in the Kindred Sayings (I, Sagāthā-vagga, Chapter VII, The Brahmin Suttas, 1, Arahats, §1, The Dhanañjāni brahminee):

> Thus have I heard:–The Exalted One was once staying near Rājagaha, in the Bamboo Grove, at the Squirrels' Feeding ground.
>
> Now at that time a Dhanañjāni brahminee, the wife of a certain brahmin of the Bhāradvāja family, was a fervent believer in the Buddha, the Dhamma and the Sangha. And she, while serving the Bhāradvāja with his dinner, came before him and uttered three times the following praise:
>
> "Glory to that Exalted One, Arahat, Buddha supreme!
> Glory to the Dhamma!
> Glory to the Sangha!"
>
> And when she had said so the Bhāradvāja brahmin exclaimed: "There now! At any and every opportunity must the wretch be speaking the praises of that shaveling friar! Now, wretch, will I give that teacher of yours a piece of my mind!"
>
> "O brahmin, I know of no one throughout the world of gods, Māras or Brahmās, recluses or brahmins, no one human or divine, who could admonish that Exalted One, Arahat, Buddha Supreme. Nevertheless, go, brahmin, and then you will know."
>
> Then the Bhāradvāja, vexed and displeased, went to find the Exalted One; and coming into his pres-

ence, exchanged with him greetings and compliments, friendly and courteous, and sat down at one side. So seated, he addressed the Exalted One in a verse:–

What must we slay if we would live happily?
What must we slay if we would weep no more?
What is it above all other things of which
The slaying you would approve, Gotama?

The Buddha said:

Wrath must you slay, if you would live happily,
Wrath must you slay, if you would weep no more.
Of anger, brahmin, with its poisoned root
And fevered tip, murderously sweet,
That is the slaying by the ariyans praised;
That must you slay in truth, to weep no more.

When the Exalted One had thus spoken, the Bhāradvāja brahmin said to him: "Most excellent, lord, most excellent."

We then read that Bhāradvāja Brahmin left the world under the Exalted One and was ordained. Not long after his ordination he attained arahatship.

Question: The Buddha spoke more in general about slaying anger, but he did not explain the way how to slay anger.

Sujin: The Buddha taught the Dhamma in many different ways and in all details so that people could see the disadvantage of akusala and the benefit of kusala. He taught the development of paññā which can slay anger completely.

Question: Anger can be slain. Through the development of vipassanā anger can be slain and through the development of samatha it can be suppressed. The development of samatha and the development of vipassanā are different, they have different aims. I have read in the "Book of Analysis", in the chapter on Jhāna (Chapter XII), that if someone wants to purify the mind of the hindrances he must sit and he must walk up and down. He must do this in order to have right effort which is necessary for the suppressing of the hindrances. Someone who develops vipassanā, however, does not have to sit or walk up and down in order to have right effort. Whenever an object appears, right understanding can know its characteristic, and then there is already right effort, which is energy for the development of understanding. Thus the development of samatha and the development of vipassanā are different. The person who develops samatha has to follow particular rules.

Sujin: Where does he begin and how does he develop it?

Question: He starts with reciting words.

Sujin: He should start with right understanding of the characteristic of the meditation subject of samatha. This subject must condition the citta to be calm, to be free from akusala. Sati sampajañña is needed to develop calm in the right way with the meditation subject.

Question: The person who develops samatha in order to attain jhāna must concentrate on the meditation subject so that calm and concentration can increase.

Sujin: That is too far-fetched, it is not related to the reality which can be experienced now, by the person who is only a beginner. Can you notice the characteristic of aversion in your daily life? The brahmin Bhāradvāja asked the Buddha, "What must we slay if we would live happily?" The Buddha answered, "Wrath must you slay if you would live happily, wrath must you slay if you would weep no more". When people are in daily life busy with their work, are there no problems and unpleasant experiences in connection with their work, with the people they meet in their work or with their colleagues? During our work we are together with other people and then there can be the arising of like and dislike, we may be distressed, annoyed, displeased or sad. Whenever you feel displeasure there is dosa, and this has many shades and degrees. We must slay dosa when it arises in the situation of our daily life, not at some other time. When we can subdue dosa in daily life there is a degree of calm or samatha. When we see the disadvantages of dosa we know that there should be mettā instead of akusala. Mettā can arise at that moment if we develop it right away and do not delay its development until later on. Thus, when there are difficult situations or when problems arise in our work, contrary to our expectations, when there are events which cause discomfort or even distress, and we can then slay dosa, there will be happiness instead of sorrow.

Question: Nobody likes aversion.

Sujin: It is in daily life that dosa should be overcome. It can be subdued by developing mettā as a meditation subject of calm, or by the development of satipaṭṭhāna. Sati of satipaṭṭhāna is mindful of the characteristics of realities which are appearing and thus paññā can be developed stage by stage, until it is so keen that the third stage of enlightenment, the stage of the anāgāmī (non-returner) can be reached and then dosa is really eradicated.

When Bhāradvāja had become a monk under the Buddha, his younger brothers heard that he had gained confidence in the Buddha and had become a monk. They became angry because of this and they gave expression to their anger in their behaviour and speech. We read in the following sutta in the Kindred Sayings (I, Chapter VII, the Brahmins, 1, Arahats, §2, Reviling):

> The Exalted One was once staying near Rājagaha, in the Bamboo Grove, near the Squirrels' Feeding-ground.
>
> Now "Reviler" of the Bhāradvāja brahmins heard that the Bhāradvāja had left the world to enter the Sangha of Gotama the Recluse. Vexed and displeased,

he sought the presence of the Exalted One, and there reviled and abused the Exalted One in rude and harsh speeches.

When he had thus spoken, the Exalted One said: "As to this, what do you think, brahmin? Do you receive visits from friends and colleagues, from relatives, by blood or marriage, from other guests?"

"Yes, Master Gotama, sometimes I do."

"As to that, what do you think, brahmin? Do you prepare for them food both dry and juicy, and an opportunity for rest?"

"Yes, Master Gotama, sometimes I do."

"But if they do not accept your hospitality, brahmin, whose do those things become?"

"If they do not accept those things, Master Gotama, they are for us."

Even so here, brahmin. That wherewith you revile us who do not revile, wherewith you scold us who do not scold, wherewith you abuse us who do not abuse, but that we do not accept from you. It is only for you, brahmin, it is only for you! He, brahmin, who reviles again at his reviler, who scolds back, who abuses in return him who has abused, this, brahmin, is as if you and your visitors dined together and made good. We neither dine together with you nor make good. It is for you only, brahmin, it is only for you!"

"The king and his court believe that Gotama the recluse is an arahat. And yet Master Gotama can indulge in wrath!"

The Exalted One said:

From where should wrath arise for him who, void of wrath,

> Holds on the even tenor of his way,
> Self-tamed, serene, by highest insight free?
> Worse of the two is he who, when reviled,
> Reviles again. Who does not, when reviled,
> Revile again, a two-fold victory wins.
> Both of the other and himself he seeks
> The good; for he the other's angry mood
> Understands and has sati and calm.
> He who of both is a physician, since
> Himself he heals and the other too,
> Those who do not know Dhamma think him a fool.
>
> When he had so said, Reviler of the Bhāradvājas spoke thus: "Most excellent, Master Gotama..."

We then read that he was ordained and not long after this became an arahat.

If we are in a similar situation, thus, when we are reviled, can mettā arise? Or must we, when someone else is angry, treat him likewise? Can we change our mood and forgive him instead of being angry in return? When there is anger, no matter whose anger it is, there is no calm, there is the wish to cause injury, to do harm. When we see the anger of someone else, his mood of wanting to do harm, and we understand the disadvantage of it, do we want to treat him likewise? When we see the disadvantage of dosa, there are conditions for the arising of mettā. We should develop mettā so that we are able to forgive someone else, even if he does wrong to us through body or speech.

We read in the following sutta in the Kindred Sayings (I, Chapter VII, Brahmin Suttas, 1, Arahats, §3, Asurinda):

> Again, while the Exalted One was at Bamboo Grove, an Asurinda Bhāradvāja brahmin also heard that the Bhāradvāja had entered the Sangha, and

> he, vexed and displeased, also went and reviled and abused the Exalted One with rude and harsh words.
>
> When he had thus spoken, the Exalted One remained silent.
>
> Then said the Asurinda: "You are conquered, recluse, you are conquered!"
>
> The Buddha said:
>
> The fool does deem the victory his
> In that he plays the bully with rude speech.
> To him who knows what forbearance is,
> This in itself makes him conqueror.
> Worse of the two is he who when reviled
> Reviles again, repays in kind.

We then read that also the Asurinda became a monk and attained arahatship.

The Buddha did not in any way retort angry words. We who still have defilements may also keep silent when we are reviled, but with what kind of cittas do we keep silent? We should consider our cittas at such moments. There are different types of cittas for the Buddha when he keeps silent, and also for the arahat, the perfected one (who has attained the fourth stage of enlightenment), for the anāgāmī (who has attained the third stage), for the sakadāgāmī (who has attained the second stage), for the sotāpanna (who has attained the first stage) and for the ordinary person: in each case there are different types of cittas at such moments. It all depends on the degree of wisdom. When someone has not yet eradicated dosa, he may keep silent and not show anger outwardly, through gestures or speech, but can we know what types of cittas he has? When satipaṭṭhāna does not arise we do not know whether we have at a particular moment kusala citta or akusala citta, we do not know whether we have true mettā. When a person who still has defilements notices that someone else keeps silent, he interprets this in accordance with his own accumulations. However, the reason of someone else's silence may be different from what he thinks.

When we carefully consider the meaning of the sutta, which was just quoted, we will see its benefit. But this also depends on the extent we live in accordance with the Dhamma. When we speak coarse words, are we the winner or the loser? Perhaps we think that we are the winner when we can speak such words to the other person, but in fact, we are the loser. If we really want to be the winner we should conquer our defilements. The person who is not angry and does not retaliate upon an angry person has won a victory which is hard to win.

When someone else is angry, we should not join him in his anger, we should not be angry with him and speak harshly to him. If we repay him in kind, we join him in his anger, we keep company with him, we keep company with akusala dhamma. Mental development is difficult, it is conditioned by listening to the teachings which explain the benefit of kusala dhammas. There must also be energy and courage in order to develop kusala dhammas. The development of all kinds of kusala is above all conditioned by satipaṭṭhāna, the development of right understanding of realities. Satipaṭṭhāna conditions the arising of sati, mindfulness, which is non-forgetful of kusala. There are different levels of sati: there is sati with generosity, with sīla (morality, the abstaining from ill deeds), with the development of calm and with the development of right understanding of realities. The development of satipaṭṭhāna can be the condition that the different levels of sati arise more often. It conditions sati to consider the disadvantage of akusala which appears, and to what extent its disadvantage is realised depends on the stage of the development of paññā. When there is sati it is paññā which can see akusala dhamma as it is. When paññā sees akusala as akusala there are conditions for the arising of kusala instead of akusala.

Another brother of Bhāradvāja expressed his anger in a way different from his brothers after he heard that the Bhāradvāja had entered the Sangha. We read in the following sutta, "The Congey-man" (Kindred Sayings I, Chapter VII, 1, §4):

> Again, while the Exalted One was at the Bamboo Grove, the Bhāradvāja brahmin, known as the Congey-man, also heard that the Bhāradvāja had entered the Sangha. And he, vexed and displeased, sought the Exalted One's presence, and when there sat at one side in silence.
>
> Then the Exalted One, discerning by his mind the thoughts of that man's mind, addressed him in verse:
>
> > Whoso does wrong to the man that's innocent,
> > Him that is pure and from all errors free,
> > His wicked act returns upon that fool
> > Like fine dust that is thrown against the wind.

Listening to the Dhamma, even for a short time, is very beneficial. When the Congey-man came to see the Buddha he was angry, although he did not scold him or blame him. However, when he considered with respect the Dhamma he heard, that is when he considered cause and effect of realities, he gained confidence in the Dhamma. He asked to be ordained under the Buddha. Not long after that he attained the supreme goal of the higher life, he became one of the arahats.

4

Mettā in daily life

Mettā-citta can arise without reciting texts about mettā. We find an example of this fact in the "Tuṇḍeila Jātaka" (III, no. 388). We read in the Commentary to this Jātaka that the Buddha told this story while he was at Jetavana.

There was a bhikkhu–a monk–who had great fear of death. He was frightened when he heard even a branch move, a stick falling or the call of a bird or another animal. The monks assembled in the Hall of Truth and spoke about that monk who was so frightened of death. They said, "now to beings in this world death is certain, life uncertain, and should this not be wisely borne in mind?"

The Buddha asked them what the subject of their conversation was and then said that bhikkhu was afraid of death not only in this life, but also in a former life.

We then read in the Tuṇḍeila Jātaka that a long time ago in Varānasī the Bodhisatta was conceived by a wild sow. In due time the sow gave birth to two male young. One day she took them to a pit where they lay down. An old woman came home from the cotton field with a basket of cotton, and was tapping the ground with her stick. The sow heard the sound and in fear of death left her young and ran away. The old woman took the two young pigs home in order to look after them and she called the bigger one, who was the Bodhisatta, Mahātuṇḍeila (big-snout) and the smaller one Cullatuṇḍeila (little-snout). She brought them up and treated them as her own children, but she loved Mahātuṇḍeila more than Cullatuṇḍeila. They grew up and became fat.

One day there were some young men who liked to eat pork meat, but they did not know where to get it. They wanted to buy the pigs from the old woman, but she said that she could not sell them since she loved them and considered them as her children. The young men did not give up and offered more money, but she did not want to sell them. Then they made her drink liquor and when she was drunk they persuaded her again to sell her pigs. She then agreed to sell only the small pig, not the big one. She took food and called Cullatuṇḍeila, the smaller pig. She had always called Mahātuṇḍeila first, and thus Mahātuṇḍeila suspected that there was danger. Cullatuṇḍeila saw that the trough was full of food and he noticed that his mistress was standing nearby and that there were also many men, with nooses in their hands. He became very frightened and did not want to eat. He ran away to his brother, shaking with fear. Mahātuṇḍeila comforted him and said that he should eat and that he should not be sad. He explained that they were fattened for their flesh's sake.

He said that all beings who are born in this world must die, that nobody could escape death. Every being, no matter whether his flesh is eatable or not eatable, must die. He said that their mother was their refuge before, but that they now had no refuge anymore. They should not have any fear and plunge in the crystal pool, to wash the stains of sweat away, they would find new ointment whose fragrance never can decay.

We read that Mahātuṇḍeila considered the ten perfections and set the perfection of mettā before him as his guide. The people who heard him preach were impressed that Mahātuṇḍeila comforted his brother and then mettā and compassion arose within them. The drunkenness left the old woman and the young men and they threw away their nooses as they stood listening to the Dhamma.

These men did not have to recite first so that mettā could arise, mettā arose because of its own conditions.

We read that Cullatuṇḍeila asked his brother,

> But what is that fair crystal pool,
> And what the stains of sweat, I pray?
> And what the ointment wonderful,
> Whose fragrance never can decay?
>
> Mahātuṇḍeila answered,
>
> Dhamma is the fair crystal pool,
> Akusala is the stain of sweat, they say:
> Virtue's the ointment wonderful,
> Whose fragrance never will decay.

Kusala dhammas are like the fair crystal pool because they can purify one from akusala which is like the stain of sweat. Sīla is like the ointment whose fragrance never can decay because when there is sīla one does not harm anybody or do anything which is disagreeable to others.

We read that Mahātuṇḍeila said that those who are fools delight in akusala, whereas those who are heedful do not take to what is unwholesome. He exhorted beings not to be sad when they had to die.

When the Buddha had told the story of the former life of that bhikkhu, he said that Mahātuṇḍeila was he himself in one of his former lives as Bodhisatta and that Cullatuṇḍeila was the bhikkhu who was afraid of death.

Thus we see that mettā can arise without reciting texts. Thinking of the words which are recited arises because of conditions. People believe that they should recite because they are used to reciting all the time. When they have such an idea it is a condition to think of the words they often recite. However, if someone develops mettā there is sati-sampajañña which considers the characteristic of mettā, and this is the opposite of akusala dhamma. When we develop mettā-citta time and again there can gradually be more mettā.

Thus, we should consider and study with awareness the characteristic of mettā as it is explained by the Buddha in many different ways. We should remember that mettā will be more powerful if it is truly developed whenever there is an opportunity for its application. Mettā can become stronger and it can arise more often if we understand the benefit of mettā. Its arising is not conditioned by the reciting of texts for a long time.

Questioner: I remember that when I was a child my father made me recite texts. I could recite many texts but I did not understand their meaning. It is the same in the case of reciting texts about mettā. The monks are chanting texts each day, in the morning and in the afternoon, and now I wonder what the use is of reciting.

Sujin: They may recite that the five khandhas are impermanent or anattā. However, the aim of reciting these words is to be reminded to consider the characteristics of the five khandhas which are appearing now and to know them as impermanent.

Question: That is true, reciting can be a reminder. When I recite, "May Mr X. be happy", I do that in order that there can be mettā for Mr X. later on.

Sujin: We read in the Visuddhimagga (Chapter IX, 1, 2) about the development of mettā from the beginning:

> To start with, he should review and try to understand the danger in hate and the advantage in patience. Why? Because hate has to be abandoned and patience attained in the development of this meditation subject and because he cannot abandon unseen dangers and attain unknown advantages.

It is not said that people should recite texts but they should know the right cause which brings the appropriate result. The "Path of Purification" (Visuddhimagga IX, 4) shows the danger of hate and the benefit of patience. If one really understands this there are, when dosa has arisen, conditions for sati-sampajañña to be aware of it immediately and to see the danger of dosa at that moment. The Visuddhimagga explains that people who begin with the development of mettā as a meditation subject of calm are advised not to develop it towards four kinds of people: a person they dislike, a dearly loved friend, a neutral person and a hostile person. Moreover, mettā should not be developed towards the opposite sex and it cannot be developed towards a dead person. It is difficult to develop mettā to the kinds of people who were just mentioned. In the beginning one is not yet ready to do that; defilements such as anger or attachment are likely to arise on account of those kinds of people. Mettā cannot be developed towards a dead person, because he is no longer the person he was before. The dying-consciousness of this life is succeeded immediately by the rebirth-consciousness of the next life and then there is a different being.

The Visuddhimagga explains that in order to make mettā grow it should first be developed towards a person one respects, someone who observes sīla, who has wisdom and other good qualities, such as one's teacher one loves and respects. The reason for this is that in the beginning mettā is not yet developed to such degree that it could be extended towards whomever one meets. In order to be able to do this it must be developed time and again, evermore.

Question: What is the proximate cause for the arising of mettā?

Sujin: Seeing the danger of dosa, aversion or hate.

Question: Can there be mettā for what is not alive?

Sujin: That is impossible. Mettā, karuṇā (compassion), muditā (sympathetic joy) and upekkhā (equanimity), which are the "four divine abidings" (brahma-vihāras), must have as object beings or people. Thus there cannot be mettā for what is not a living being. However, as regards dosa, aversion, there can be aversion not only towards beings, but also towards things or circumstances.

Question: Can mettā arise just after seeing a visible object?

Sujin: Mettā has beings as object. When you see a small child can there not be mettā? How will you act when there is mettā? You may speak in a kind way, you may help the child to cross the street. This is the way to develop mettā. We can realise ourselves to what extent mettā is already developed. We cannot expect mettā to arise if we do not know its characteristic.

Question: What is the difference between mettā which arises just after seeing and mettā which arises while we are thinking?

Sujin: When you see beings and people and you are annoyed you can be aware of this. After seeing there may be akusala or there may be mettā. When there is mettā you consider the other person as a friend, you wish for his happiness and want to do everything which is beneficial for him. You feel happy and cheerful while you think of his well-being, you may smile and you will not behave in any way which will make him unhappy.

Also when you give him something you can do that in such a way that it truly makes him happy. There are many ways of giving things to others. Some people give in such a way that the other person feels no joy when he receives something. When mettā has already become more developed, when it has become stronger, it conditions our actions and speech and also our way of thinking about other people. Even when we do not see other people we can think of them with kindness. We can think of promoting their well-being and happiness, we can consider ways to help particular persons, to support them in different ways. Then there is mettā, without the need to recite texts.

Reciting texts on mettā is actually not so difficult, but truly developing mettā is difficult. This cannot be accomplished by reciting texts. As I said before, there must be sati-sampajañña in daily life which knows precisely the characteristic of mettā. It must know precisely when there is kusala citta and when akusala citta.

Question: I think that one should recite in the beginning.

Sujin: You said the same about the development of satipaṭṭhāna, you said that one should think before there can be awareness. You know that seeing is the reality which experiences, the element which experiences, and that the object which appears, visible object, is only a physical reality which can be experienced through the eyes. Sometimes you believe that you need to repeat to yourself that seeing is the reality, the element, which experiences through the eyes, and that the object which appears is a physical reality, rūpa-dhamma, which is experienced through the eyes. When there is hearing of a sound you believe that you should repeat this to yourself first, because you think that the reciting of words is very useful. What you should understand correctly first of all is that each reality arises because of its appropriate conditions. There are also conditions for thinking to arise more often than sammā-sati, right awareness. When sammā-sati arises it can be directly aware of the realities which appear; it can consider them in the right way, so that they can be understood as non-self.

As to the term sammā-sati, sammā can be translated as right, and sati is awareness or mindfulness. Sammā-sati is aware in the right way, considers realities in the right way. How is it aware in the right way? When there is seeing there can be right mindfulness of the characteristic of the rūpa-dhamma which appears through the eyes, which is different from nāma-dhamma. There can be right mindfulness of nāma-dhamma, the reality which experiences, the element which experiences, which is seeing. Then there is sammā-sati which is mindful in the right way, which is directly aware of the characteristic of the reality which appears. If people believe that they should recite, they will continue to do that, instead of being directly aware of the characteristic of nāma or of the characteristic of rūpa. If one sees realities as they are, as non-self, anattā, one will know that thinking about reciting, thinking about words one repeats to oneself, is only a reality which arises because of its own conditions. At such a moment sammā-sati cannot yet be directly aware of the characteristics of nāma-dhammas and rūpa-dhammas, and thus there is not yet precise knowledge of them. There is only thinking about the characteristics of realities which appear, thus, there is only theoretical understanding of them. If paññā realises this there can be the development of sammā-sati, instead of thinking of reciting or naming realities "nāma" and "rūpa", of repeating this to oneself. Sammā-sati is directly aware of realities and considers in the right way the characteristics of nāma and rūpa.

There is no rule at all in the development of satipaṭṭhāna. When someone thinks about the names of realities or thinks that he should recite words in order to remind himself, he should remember that thinking in this way arises because of conditions. He cannot force himself not to think in this way. However, thinking is not sammā-sati of the eightfold Path. When sammā-sati of the eightfold Path arises, it is aware in the right way of the characteristics of nāma and rūpa and at that moment sammā-diṭṭhi, right understanding, can investigate the true nature of nāma and rūpa. Thus paññā can grow and it can realise nāma and rūpa as they are: not a being, not a person, not self.

In daily life we see beings, we see people who belong to different families, who are different as to the colour of their skin, who have a different rank or position in society, who speak different languages, and who behave in different ways. When we think of people who are so different in many ways and we have right understanding of the characteristic of mettā, sati-sampajañña can arise and be aware of the characteristic of the citta which thinks. Then it can be known what type of citta is thinking, mettā-citta or akusala citta. When akusala citta thinks of people, it can be realised as such. For instance the akusala citta which is rooted in attachment, lobha-mūla-citta, may be accompanied by conceit or it may be without conceit. Sometimes we think of others with conceit, and sometimes we think only with attachment but without conceit. Or there may be akusala citta which is rooted in aversion, dosa-mūla-citta. We may think of others with aversion or even anger. Dosa-mūla-citta may at times be accompanied by avarice or by jealousy. Thus we see that there are different types of akusala cittas which may think of other people. The understanding of our different cittas can arise again and again so that it grows and this is a condition for the arising of mettā when we see people or when we think of people in daily life. In that way mettā can develop more and more, and there can eventually be mettā for all beings. If people want to develop mettā as a meditation subject which can condition calm, they cannot do this without precise knowledge of the different cittas which arise. There must be right understanding which knows exactly the characteristic of calm which accompanies mettā when it appears at a particular moment in daily life. When there is calm there are at such moments no defilements.

Question: Reciting, repeating words aloud is useful. When

there is seeing, I say to myself that this is colour, the reality which appears through eyes, or that is the nāma which sees.

Sujin: I do not say that it is not useful, but it is not sammā-sati of the eightfold Path, and moreover, there is no rule that one should recite words. Some people believe that there is a rule that they should recite words and they cling to this idea. There is attachment instead of sammā-sati which considers in the right way the characteristics of nāma and rūpa. When people think that the reciting of words is useful, they continue to do this again and again. They should not forget, however, that reciting, the repeating of words, arises because of its appropriate conditions and that it is not yet sammā-sati. People should find out for themselves what is more useful, reciting or sammā-sati of the eightfold Path which considers in the right way the characteristics of nāma and rūpa at the moments one does not recite.

Question: Sammā-sati is certainly better, but my paññā is not yet developed to that degree.

Sujin: This shows that there are conditions for thinking about realities. However, at such a moment paññā should also know that there is not yet sammā-sati of the eightfold Path. When there are at a particular moment conditions for sammā-sati which is directly aware of nāma and rūpa, you can find out that the right understanding which can develop at that very moment is not the same as the reciting of words.

Question: If I recite words over and over, for a long time, sati can arise often and then I can investigate realities with understanding.

Sujin: This is understanding of the level of thinking, it is intellectual understanding. There is not yet direct awareness of the characteristics of nāma and rūpa. You spend a lot of time reciting, repeating words, but it would be better if there could be sammā-sati which begins to be aware in the right way of the characteristics of some nāmas and rūpas, little by little. Even though there is not yet precise knowledge of the characteristics of nāma and rūpa and there is not yet clear understanding of their true nature, you can begin to be mindful of their characteristics. Thus it can gradually become one's inclination to be mindful of the realities which appear. The arising of sammā-sati depends on conditions, but when it arises there is direct awareness of nāma and rūpa and this is more useful than the reciting of words.

Question: That is right. If there can be awareness and direct understanding of the reality which appears as rūpa or as nāma, paññā has developed already to a certain level. However, when someone is a beginner, paññā has not reached that level yet.

Sujin: Those who are beginners have different accumulations. If people have right understanding of the characteristic of sammā-sati, it can arise. One may not yet be accomplished in the development of paññā, but one knows the characteristic of sammā-sati, the reality which is mindful and directly aware of the nāma which sees or hears or the rūpa which appears through one of the senses or the mind. When there is right awareness the characteristic of the reality which appears can be studied and investigated. It is true that we cannot prevent thinking from arising, but we should not cling to it and believe that it is a rule that we should think of words for a long time and repeat them to ourselves in order that sammā-sati can arise afterwards.

5

Characteristic of mettā

The development of satipaṭṭhāna is not repeating words to oneself, or naming realities "nāma" and "rūpa", without investigating the characteristics of the realities which appear. This becomes clearer when we read the "Velāma sutta" (Gradual Sayings, Book of the Nines, Chapter II, §10). We read that the Buddha, while he was near Sāvatthī, at the Jeta Grove, spoke to Anāthapiṇḍeika about the gifts given by him in a former life, when he was the brahmin Velāma. He compared the value of different good deeds:

> ...though with a heart full of confidence he took refuge in the Buddha, the Dhamma and the Sangha, greater would have been the fruit thereof, had he with confidence undertaken to keep the precepts: abstention from taking life, from taking what is not

> given, from carnal lusts, from lying and from intoxicating liquor, the cause of sloth.
>
> ... though with confidence he undertook to keep these precepts, greater would have been the fruit thereof, had he developed a mere passing fragrance of mettā.
>
> ... though he developed just the fragrance of mettā, greater would have been the fruit thereof, had he developed, just for a finger-snap, aniccā-saññā, the perception of impermanence.

Thus we see that the development of satipaṭṭhāna is of the greatest value, since through satipaṭṭhāna the characteristics of realities are seen as they are.

Mettā is one of the four brahma-vihāras, divine abidings. The development of mettā is intricate and one should learn about it in detail. The Buddha explained that mettā should be developed time and again so that it can grow. When mettā has been developed, it can also support the development of the other brahma-vihāras of compassion, sympathetic joy and equanimity. When someone has developed mettā, he can have compassion: he will not hurt other beings. He can have sympathetic joy: he will rejoice in other people's happiness. Whereas if one does not develop mettā one is likely to hurt other beings and one will not rejoice in their happiness. The Buddha stressed that the development of mettā is very beneficial, since mettā conditions the arising of other kusala dhammas. Therefore it is important to consider the development of mettā more in detail.

If someone thinks that he can develop mettā by the recitation of texts about mettā, he should try to find out whether this is the right approach.

Question: It is written that one should recite: "May all beings be free from misfortune, may they be free from sorrow and unhappiness, may they live in happiness. ”

Sujin: You wish this for all beings, don’t you?

Question: That is right. This is actually the extension of mettā. I have learnt the Pāli text, but since I do not know the meaning I use the Thai translation for my recitation. In this way I can understand the words I recite.

I think that while I am reciting there is sati. Sometimes it happens that I am reciting and then, without realizing it, I do not go on with the reciting. I am at times distracted and I think of other things. But at other moments I realise that I am reciting and that I should not think of other things. When I notice that I stop reciting is there then sati? When there is sati I can start again from the beginning with the recitation of the text.

Sujin: You extend mettā to all beings, but have you attained jhāna already? If that is not so how can you extend mettā to all beings? When there is mettā the citta is calm. When you think of a person you dislike, a person you love or a neutral person and there is no calm at such moments, how can you extend mettā to all beings? As the Visuddhimagga explains, in the beginning it is difficult to have mettā for a person one dislikes, a person one loves or a neutral person. When you recite that you wish happiness for all beings can you truly extend mettā to all beings? You can only have boundless mettā, including all beings, no matter where they are, if you have attained jhāna.

People should not believe that they, when they begin to develop mettā, can truly, wholeheartedly, wish happiness to all beings. When they really know themselves, they can find out that they do not mean this. When they think of someone they dislike mettā does not arise. Are they then sincere when they recite that they wish happiness for all beings? As we have seen, the attainment of jhāna is necessary in order to be able to extend mettā to all beings.

When we think of a person we like, attachment is likely to

arise and this is not mettā. When we think of someone we hate or of someone who is a hostile person there is no calm and we are simply not sincere when we recite for ourselves the text of the mettā sutta: "May all beings be happy". If someone wants to develop calm, he should remember that calm is a wholesome quality arising with kusala citta. When kusala citta arises there are no defilements and then there is calm. If the characteristic of calm is known, it can grow, stage by stage. Mettā is a meditation subject of samatha which can condition the growth of calm, and it can also condition moments of calm in daily life. However, in order to develop mettā in the right way, it is not sufficient to think of mettā, but we should know first of all the characteristic of mettā. It is actually the same as in the case of the development of satipaṭṭhāna. We cannot develop it if we do not know the characteristic of sati, mindfulness. We may take thinking for mindfulness but thinking is different from mindfulness. Sati of satipaṭṭhāna is not forgetful, it is directly aware of the reality which appears at the present moment and it considers the characteristic of that reality. For the development of mettā mindfulness is necessary. If there is mindfulness of mettā when it appears, its characteristic can be known through direct experience.

We read in the Atthasālinī (II, Book II, Part II, The Summary, II, 362) about adosa, non-aversion. The Atthasālinī, which is a commentary to the Dhammasangaṇi, the first book of the Abhidhamma, explains in this context the terms used in the Dhammasangaṇi to define the reality of adosa:

> "...having love" is exercising love, "loving" is the method of exercising love; lovingness is the nature of citta which is endowed with love, is productive of love. Tender care is watchfulness, the meaning is that one protects. Tenderly caring is the method of such care. Tender carefulness is the state of tenderly

caring. Beneficence is seeking to do good. "Compassion" is the exercising of compassion...

Before mettā can be developed we should first of all become familiar with the characteristic of mettā. We should carefully consider the nature of our citta at this moment: is it really accompanied by mettā or not? In this way we can begin to develop mettā very gradually, by showing kindness to someone else, and then mettā can increase.

We should consider the words of the Atthasālinī about friendship and the attitude of intimacy, of closeness. When we are sitting together with others, do we have a kind disposition towards them, do we have sincere friendship? If that is the case, we can learn what the characteristic of mettā is.

No matter whether we meet people in a room, or outside, on the street or in the bus, do we consider everybody we meet as a friend? If that is not so we should not recite the words about extending mettā to all beings–that will not be of any use. If we see someone now, at this moment, and we feel misgivings about him, we should not try to extend mettā to all beings. Only those who have attained jhāna are able to do this. When the meditation subject of mettā brahma-vihāra has been developed mettā, can become boundless. However, we should begin with simply applying sincere mettā in daily life.

Question: My aim is not jhāna-citta, I do not expect to attain jhāna.

Sujin: Therefore mettā cannot yet be extended to all beings.

Question: I recite the words about extending mettā to all beings with the aim to have kusala citta.

Sujin: But when you see a hostile person or when you think of him annoyance is likely to arise.

Question: Yes, that is possible.

Sujin: Therefore you should not try to extend mettā to all beings, because you don't mean it.

Question: I think that it is useful because while I am reciting the citta is kusala.

Sujin: This is not possible if you do not start in the right way, that is, knowing the true characteristic of mettā.

Question: It is stated in the Visuddhimagga that one should begin with extending mettā towards oneself.

Sujin: In the beginning people are not yet ready to extend mettā to others and therefore they can take themselves as an example. They can remind themselves that they should treat others in the same way as they would like to be treated themselves. That is the meaning of extending mettā towards oneself.

Question: Thus the aim is to sympathise?

Sujin: To sympathise with other people.

Question: Thus we have to extend mettā towards ourselves, towards a disagreeable person, towards a loved person and towards a neutral person.

Sujin: If you cannot yet have mettā for a disagreeable person, you cannot extend mettā at all. If you try to extend mettā towards a dearly loved person, attachment is likely to arise and attachment has a characteristic which is different from the characteristic of mettā. Thus in that case you are not successful either. Towards whom should we first extend mettā?

Question: I think towards oneself.

Sujin: This is said only by way of reminder as we have seen. Those who are beginners and not yet accomplished should think of someone else who excels in sīla, who has many good qualities which inspire love and respect. It can be one's teacher or someone who is the equivalent of one's teacher, someone who is full of mettā and other kusala dhammas. When we think of such a person our citta becomes soft and malleable and we can then be intent on ways to have kusala citta. We will do everything we can for the benefit and wellbeing of that person. That is how we can begin with the development of mettā.

The Visuddhimagga (IX, 93) states about the characteristic, function, manifestation and proximate cause of mettā:

> Mettā has the characteristic of promoting the aspect of welfare. Its function is to prefer welfare. It is manifested as the removal of annoyance. Its proximate cause is seeing lovableness in beings. It succeeds when it makes ill-will subside, and it fails when it produces selfish affection.

It is difficult to be watchful as to our cittas, because we are so used to having akusala. Attachment, aversion and ignorance arise time and again. In order to develop kusala, paññā, right understanding of realities, is necessary. There must be sati-sampajañña which knows the characteristic of the citta at a particular moment, which knows whether there is kusala citta or akusala citta. When we sincerely wish to do something for another person, not because of attachment, not because he belongs to our circle of friends or relatives, not because we expect affection in return, there is the characteristic of mettā.

In order to develop mettā we should have a detailed knowledge of our cittas, we should carefully consider the different cittas which arise. It is in daily life that we can truly develop mettā, when there is sati-sampajañña which knows the characteristic of mettā which appears. We may happen to see someone who has a peculiar appearance, or someone who is a foreigner, someone who speaks a different language. How do we feel at such a moment? Do we have the same feeling as if we see a friend or do we have a feeling of antipathy? If we consider that person, whomever he may be, as a true friend, there is the manifestation of mettā. As we have seen in the definition of mettā in the Visuddhimagga, the manifestation of mettā is the removal of annoyance, of displeasure.

When we see two people who are angry with each other or who quarrel and we are partial to one of them there is no mettā but lobha. As we have seen in the definition, when there is selfish affection the development of mettā fails. We can consider the two people who are angry with one another as friends, it does not matter who of the two acted in the proper way and who in the wrong way. When we see someone who treated us badly, we can still have mettā towards him, we can try to help him and we can think of his well-being. Then there is true mettā which arises at such a moment. There is no mettā if we are annoyed with the person who treated us badly, if we blame him and cause him to be even more upset.

If someone has mettā he considers everybody as his friend. If there is a sincere feeling of friendship for others there can also be compassion, karuṇā, when someone else has to experience sorrow and misfortune. If someone else experiences happiness, if he has prosperity and success, there can be sympathetic joy, muditā. If we try to help someone but that person cannot be relieved from distress, we can develop the brahma-vihāra of equanimity, upekkhā, and then we will not have aversion about the suffering of that person. We can understand that all dhammas are dependant on their appropriate conditions. The person who has to suffer receives the result of the kamma he performed.

The four brahma-vihāras are excellent qualities which support all other kinds of wholesome deeds so that these can develop and reach perfection. The brahma-vihāras can support, for example, generosity. When an opportunity for giving presents itself, we can give without partiality, whereas when we do not develop the brahma-vihāras we may be inclined to give only to a particular group of people. The brahma-vihāras are a condition for the perfecting of sīla, good moral conduct through action and speech. We can perform kusala without expecting favours in return. We can forgive other people, whatever harm they did to us. Mettā can indeed support the other brahma-vihāras of compassion, sympathetic joy and equanimity, if the right conditions and the proximate causes for the other brahma-vihāras are present.

We read in the Gradual Sayings (Book of the Fives, Chapter XVII, §1, The putting away of Malice) that the Buddha teaches that we should develop all four brahma-vihāras. We should not believe that mettā should first be developed to a high degree and that after that the other three brahma-vihāras can be developed. The text states:

> Monks, there are five ways of putting away malice whereby all malice arisen in a monk ought to be put away. What five?
>
> Monks, in whatsoever person malice is engendered, in him loving-kindness ought to be made to become more. In this way malice in him ought to be put away.
>
> Monks, in whomsoever malice is engendered, in him compassion... equanimity ought to be made to become more. In this way malice in him ought to be put away.
>
> Monks, in whomsoever malice is engendered, in that man unmindfulness, inattention to it, ought to be brought about. In this way malice in him ought to be put away.
>
> Monks, in whomsoever malice is engendered he should remember that people are owners of their deeds. This should be firmly established in his mind. He should think: This, reverend sir, is of one's own making, he is the heir of his deeds, deeds are the matrix, deeds are the kin, deeds are the foundation; whatever one does, good or bad, one will become heir to that. In this way malice in him ought to be put away.

> Verily, monks, these are the five ways of putting away malice.

It is natural that we are annoyed or irritated about certain people, that we find them disagreeable. Dosa may be strong and it may last for a long time, or it may be less intense and disappear soon. We should remember that even when coarse dosa, such as malice or ill-will arises, it can be subdued by the development of the four brahma-vihāras.

We read in the following sutta (Gradual Sayings, Book of the Fives, Chapter XVII, §2) that the venerable Sāriputta said to the monks that, when anger arises, one should have wise consideration of the different people one is angry with. People are different as to their conduct through body, speech and mind. Some people may perform good deeds through the body, but their speech and thoughts are akusala. Some people perform akusala kamma (bad deeds) through body and mind but their speech is wholesome. Some people are impure as to their actions through body and speech but they can have mental calm, they listen to the Dhamma and they are interested in it. Although they develop calm their impurity as to body or speech appears from time to time. We can think of these people without anger, annoyance can be subdued by the development of mettā. There can be mettā when we think only of someone's good qualities which appear, we should not pay attention to what he does wrong because then we will have aversion.

It can happen that someone is gentle in his behaviour and that he has agreeable speech but that his way of thinking is not in accordance with his conduct through body and speech. When we know this we should pay attention only to his good qualities, his wholesome conduct through body and speech, and then mettā can arise. Some people may have compassion when they think of someone else, they think of his good qualities, for example, his wholesome conduct through body and speech, or, if he has bad conduct through body and speech but he has mental calm, they think of that quality. They may have compassion and may wish to help the other person. This shows that they have made progress with the development of the brahma-vihāras. We may not be angry with someone else, but can there be compassion, do we really wish to help him if he is in trouble? Can we have sympathetic joy when someone with whom we were annoyed has prosperity, honour, praise and happiness? If people can rejoice at such an occasion it shows that they have made progress with the development of the brahma-vihāras.

In the "Mettā-sutta" (Gradual Sayings, Book of the Fours, Chapter XIII, §5) we read about the results of the development of the four brahma-vihāras. When someone develops calm and attains jhāna with mettā as meditation subject and the jhāna does not decline, he is reborn in the plane of the "Devas of the Brahma-group" and there the life-span is about one kappa. When someone develops jhāna with compassion as subject and the jhāna does not decline he is reborn in the plane of the "Radiant Devas" and there the life-span is about two kappas. When someone develops jhāna with sympathetic joy as subject and the jhāna does not decline, he is reborn in the plane of the "Ever-radiant Devas" and there the life-span is about four kappas. When someone develops jhāna with equanimity as subject and the jhāna does not decline he is reborn in the plane of the "Vehapphala Devas" and there the life-span is about five hundred kappas.

The development of mettā has many benefits and it supports other ways of kusala, such as the "ways of showing sympathy", which are: liberality, kindly speech, beneficial actions and impartiality, as explained in the teachings. Mettā conditions generosity in giving and it conditions kind, agreeable speech. It makes one abstain from rude, disgracious conduct, from doing wrong to others. We can help people with kindness and we can consider them as fellow-beings who are friends. We can learn not to think of them with conceit, as strangers who are different. We will learn not to think of them in terms of "he" and "me", or to consider them as superior or as inferior in comparison with ourselves, because that is conceit. When we investigate the characteristic of our citta we will know from our own experience that kusala citta is completely different from akusala citta.

The Dhammasangaṇi (Buddhist Psychological Ethics, the first book of the Abhidhamma, §1340) refers to wholesome qualities such as plasticity, gentleness, smoothness, pliancy, and humbleness of heart. The commentary to this passage (Atthasālinī II, Book III, 395) describes humbleness of heart as follows:

> "by the absence of conceit this person's heart is humble; the state of such a person is humbleness of heart."

Softness, gentleness, pliancy and humbleness of heart, these qualities are characteristics of mettā. Sāriputta was an example of humility. He compared himself with a dust rag, an old rag without any value. He had no arrogance, he was not conceited about it that he was one of the foremost disciples. Even when others behaved badly towards him through body or speech he was unaffected by it since he was an arahat. He had eradicated conceit and all the other defilements and thus he was of perfect gentleness and humility.

Can we have true humility? When there is unwholesomeness in our actions and speech we should be mindful of the characteristic of citta at such moments. We can find out that we are full of defilements and that these condition our behaviour and speech. When there is sincere humility there cannot be unwholesome speech. Our behaviour and our speech reflect our citta: kusala citta or akusala citta. Is there mettā or is there conceit? If we want to strive earnestly for the eradication of defilements we should be mindful of the different cittas. Then we will notice what our normal behaviour and speech is in our daily life. We will know when they are motivated by akusala citta and when by kusala citta.

6

Mettā in action and speech

Mettā supports other kusala dhammas, it is also a condition for patience. We read in the Dhammasangaṇi:

> §1341: What is patience (khanti)?
>
> That patience which is long-suffering, compliance, absence of rudeness and abruptness, complacency of citta.
>
> §1342: What is temperance (soraccaṃ)?
>
> That which is the absence of excess in deed, in word, and in deed and word together. Besides, all moral self-restraint (saṁvara sīla) is temperance.
>
> §1343: What is amity (sākhalyaṃ)?
>
> When all such speech as is insolent, disagreeable, scabrous, harsh to others, vituperative to others, bordering upon anger, not conducive to concentration,

> is put away, and when all such speech as is innocuous, pleasant to the ear, affectionate, such as goes to the heart, is urbane, sweet and acceptable to people generally; when speech of this sort is spoken, polished, friendly and gentle speech, this is what is called amity.

We read in the Atthasālinī (Book II, Part II, Chapter II, 396) the following explanation of the passage on amity in the Dhammasaṅgaṇi:

> In the exposition of amity, "insolent" means, as knobs protrude in a decaying or unhealthy tree, so, owing to faultiness, knobs are produced from words of abusing and slandering, etc. "Scabrous" means putrid, like a putrid tree. As a putrid tree is scabrous and has trickling, powdery tissue, so such speech is scabrous and enters as though piercing the ear. "Harsh to others" means bitter to the ears of others, not pleasant to their hearts and productive of dosa. "Vituperative to others" means, as a branch with barbed thorns sticks by penetrating into leather, so it sticks to others and clings on, hindering those who want to go. "Bordering on anger" means near to anger. "Not conducive to concentration" means not conducive to attainment-concentration (appanā-samādhi) and access-concentration. All these terms are synonyms of the words "with hate"...
>
> "Pleasant to the ear", that is, from sweetness of diction, it is pleasant to the ear; it does not produce pain to the ear, like the piercing of a needle. And from the sweetness of sense and meaning not producing ill-temper in the body, it produces affection, and so is called "affectionate". That speech which appeals to the heart, which enters the mind easily

> without striking, we say "goes to the heart". "Urbane speech" is so called because it is full of good qualities, and because it is refined like well-bred persons, and because it is of the town (urban). It means talk of citizens. For these use appropriate speech and address fatherly men as fathers, and brotherly men as brothers. "Of-much-folk-sweetness" means sweet to many people. "Of-much-folk-pleasantness" means pleasant to many people and making for the growth of mind. "The speech which there", that is, in that person, "is gentle", i.e. polished, "friendly", that is soft, "smooth", that is, not harsh.

In connection with amity there is another term, namely "courtesy" (patisanthāro). One should not merely have speech which is blameless, pleasant to the ears, affectionate, which goes to the heart and which is urbane. It is important to have also courtesy through loving-kindness. When one really develops mettā one is not without courtesy. We read in the Dhammasangaṇi:

> §1344: What is courtesy (patisanthāro)?
>
> The two forms of courtesy: hospitality towards bodily needs and considerateness in matters of the Dhamma. When anyone shows courtesy it is in one or other of these two forms.

There cannot be real courtesy if there is no mettā. When there is sincere courtesy in daily life it is evident that there is mettā-citta. If we do not have courtesy in our daily life we should develop mettā so that we can help other people with courtesy in our deeds and speech.

The Atthasālinī (397) explains the term courtesy:

> In the exposition of courtesy, "carnal courtesy" (āmisa patisanthāro) is the closing, covering up, by means

> of bodily needs, the gap which might exist between oneself and others owing to those needs not getting satisfied.

Thus, this refers to helping others by giving them things they need, by looking after them. There is a gap or separation between people all the time, between those who possess things and those who are needy. However, there is a means to close such a gap and that is by material courtesy, by giving assistance with material things, helping those in need. Then there is no longer a separation or distance between people.

As to "Dhamma courtesy" (dhamma patisanthāro), this is the closing of the gap which might exist between oneself and others who did not learn the Dhamma. When we see the benefit of the Dhamma and we think it appropriate to help others by explaining the Dhamma there is courtesy of Dhamma. Then the Dhamma covers completely the gap or separation between people.

We read further on in the Atthasālinī (398) about material courtesy of the monk:

> A courteous bhikkhu, on seeing a guest arrive, should meet him and take his bowl and robe, offer him a seat, fan him with Palmyra leaf, wash his feet, rub him with oil; if there be butter and syrup he should give him medicine, offer him water, scour up the monastery –thus, in one part is material courtesy shown.

Lay-followers should consider by which means they can in their own situation show material courtesy. As to Dhamma courtesy by which people can help one another, we read in the Atthasālinī:

> Moreover, at eventide, if there be no junior who comes to pay his respects, the bhikkhu should go to the

> presence of his guest, sit there and, without asking him irrelevant things, question him on relevant things. He should not ask "What texts do you recite? but should ask "What scriptural text does your teacher and spiritual adviser use?" and should question him on points within his capacities. Should the guest be able to answer, that is good; if not, he himself should give the reply. Thus in one part is courtesy of Dhamma shown.

This shows that there is thoughtfulness when we speak with mettā. When we want to help others with Dhamma we should not explain what is beyond the listener's capacity to understand or to receive. We should take into consideration the accumulations and the disposition of the listener and speak about the Dhamma in such a way that he can understand it.

Mettā supports other kusala dhammas and it has many benefits. If we know about these benefits we can verify for ourselves whether mettā is already of such degree that we can have them. Thus, reading about them can remind us to develop mettā to that degree.

We read in the "Mettā-sutta" (Gradual Sayings, Book of the Eights, Chapter I, §1):

> Thus have I heard:
>
> Once the Exalted One was dwelling near Sāvatthī, at Jeta Grove, in Anāthapiṇḍeika's Park. There the Exalted One addressed the monks, saying: "Monks".
>
> "Yes, lord, " they replied, and the Exalted One said:
>
> Monks, by the release of the heart through mettā (mettā cetovimutti), practised, made become, made much of, made a vehicle and a basis, exercised, augmented and set going, eight advantages are to be expected. What eight?

> Happy one sleeps; happy one awakes; one sees no bad dreams; one is dear to humans; one is dear to non-humans; devas guard one; neither fire, nor poison, nor sword affects one; and though one penetrate not the beyond, one reaches the Brahmā world.
>
> Monks, by the release of the heart through amity, practised, made become, made much of, made a vehicle and a basis, exercised, augmented and set going, these eight advantages are to be expected.

> Who does make mettā to grow
> Boundless and thereto sets his mind,
> Seeing the end of birth's substrate
> In him the fetters are worn away.
> If with a heart unsoiled one feels
> Mettā towards a single being,
> He is a good man (just) by that.
> Compassionate of heart to all
> The ariyan boundless merit makes.
> Those royal sages who, conquering
> The creature teeming earth, have ranged
> Round and about with sacrifice...
> Such do not share a sixteenth part
> The worth of mettā-citta made to grow,
> Just as the radiance of the moon
> Outshines all the starry host.
> Who kills not nor makes others kill,
> Robs not nor makes others rob,
> Sharing goodwill with all that lives,
> He has no hate for anyone.

One of the benefits of the development of mettā is that one sleeps happily. If we are angry with someone can we then sleep happily? If we are not angry with anyone, if we have no hate and we can forgive anybody whatever wrong he may have done, we can really sleep happily. If sati-sampajañña arises when it is time to go to sleep, we can find out what type of citta arises before falling asleep. We can find out whether there is at such a moment lobha, dosa, satipaṭṭhāna or mettā. If we develop satipaṭṭhāna, there can be paññā which knows the characteristics of realities as they are. When the reality which appears at a particular moment is akusala, sati-sampajañña (paññā arising with sati) can realise akusala as akusala. Paññā can distinguish the difference between kusala dhamma and akusala dhamma and thus it is able to eliminate akusala more and more. The development of kusala is the only way to have the benefit of sleeping happily.

Waking up happily is another benefit. When it is time to get up in the morning we can find out whether mettā has been sufficiently developed so that we can have this benefit. If there is anger remaining in our heart, the citta will be disturbed when we wake up; we are preoccupied with events we can't forget. In reality, there is no self, being or person, but there are conditions for citta to be disturbed. As soon as we wake up saññā (remembrance) remembers the event which causes us to be annoyed. Or when we have done something wrong and we worry because of this, we cannot help thinking of this as soon as we wake up. When we have done something wrong we are likely to worry about it and to feel unhappy when we go to sleep, and then we are also unhappy when we wake up. When there is akusala citta before going to sleep there will also be akusala citta as soon as we wake up. When there is akusala citta rooted in lobha, and there is no mindfulness of it, we will not realise it that there is clinging as soon as we wake up. There is clinging to the objects which appear through eyes, ears, nose, tongue, body-sense and mind-door. We usually do not notice attachment to the sense objects when it is of a slight degree and we do not see its disadvantage and danger.

Dosa is a reality which is more coarse and thus it is less

difficult to realise it as akusala than in the case of lobha. When there is dosa the citta is disturbed and unhappy. Lobha is not coarse and fierce like dosa, it is difficult to realise it as akusala. If we develop satipaṭṭhāna naturally, in daily life, we will know the characteristics of realities just as they are, we will know when there is lobha and when there is dosa.

One of the benefits of the development of mettā is not having bad dreams. Unwholesome, impure thoughts can arise even in dreams, they cannot be prevented. Our accumulated inclinations condition the arising of cittas in mind-door processes which think about the objects which were formerly experienced through the six doors. We remember all these objects and dwell on them with our thoughts. People's accumulated defilements condition different dreams. We can sometimes know whether there were kusala cittas or akusala cittas while we were dreaming. Then we can scrutinise ourselves as to our accumulations, we can see whether kusala or akusala has been accumulated. If one has accumulated a great deal of mettā one will not have bad dreams, thus, there will not be akusala citta which dreams.

"One is dear to humans" is another benefit of the development of mettā. Do we know of ourselves whether we are usually liked by others? When we investigate the characteristics of our cittas we can know why we are liked or disliked by others. Some people blame kamma of the past for the fact that, although they do all kinds of good deeds they are still not liked by other people. Therefore they feel slighted and disappointed. Other people can hurt or harm us only through their actions and speech. When they speak in a disagreeable way, the rūpa which is ear-sense is a condition to hear different sounds which can disturb us. However, in reality our citta cannot be harmed by someone else at all, it can only be harmed by ourselves. Other people can only cause us to have bodily suffering; it is our own akusala citta which is the cause of mental suffering. Thus, instead of thinking of all the different things which cause us to be distressed we should cultivate mettā and we should forgive other people. Then the citta is not disturbed and it is evident that nobody can do harm to our citta.

We want to be dear to others but we may forget that we ourselves should also show affection to other people. We should not expect that other people will first show kindness and affection; there should be no delay in being kind and considerate to others. At such moments we have no sadness or worry. The citta with mettā is kusala, at that moment there is no lobha, no wish to have affection from someone else in return.

If one knows the characteristic of kusala citta and discerns the difference between kusala citta and akusala citta there are conditions to develop a great deal of kusala without being concerned about it whether one is liked by other people or not. When there is mettā and generosity, when one helps other people, there is the cetasika chanda, "wish-to-do", which conditions the arising of kusala citta. The desire for kusala is different from lobha. When lobha arises we desire to be liked by others. Whereas when kusala chanda arises, we desire to develop loving kindness towards others, even when we do not receive any kindness from them.

If satipaṭṭhāna is not developed, we cannot clearly distinguish between the different characteristics of lobha and of kusala chanda which desires the development of kusala. There may be attachment to the development of kusala or to the benefits of kusala because clinging cannot yet be eliminated. We know that good deeds bring their appropriate results but when we have expectations, when we hope that our good deeds will bring pleasant results, there is lobha. When there is kusala chanda, desire for the development of kusala, there is no attachment, there are no expectations with regard to the result of kusala. Then we can develop kusala with a sincere inclination, we can develop it naturally and spontaneously.

"One is dear to non-humans", this is another benefit of the

development of mettā. When there is chanda, desire for the development of kusala, we do not expect to be liked by human beings nor by non-humans, because we do not hope for the result of kusala, we do not hope for any benefit. When there is pure kusala one is dear to non-humans.

"Devas guard one", this is another benefit. When we develop mettā, kusala citta has as effect that we are dear to humans and non-humans and that devas guard us with mettā. The right cause brings its appropriate effect, and there is no need to wish for such result.

"Neither fire, nor poison nor sword affects one", this is another benefit. When there is pure kusala citta with mettā, it can protect us from dangers, even if we have not attained "access concentration" or jhāna. When someone develops calm with mettā as meditation subject and his kusala citta is of such degree of steadfastness that jhāna can be attained, he will not be affected by fire, poison or sword.

"Even when one does not reach the highest, one will be reborn in the Brahmā world", this is another benefit, which, as I shall explain, shows clearly that satipaṭṭhāna should be developed together with all the other kinds of kusala. When someone develops samatha with mettā as subject, and he can attain calm which is steadfast, and which is of the degree that the first jhāna can be reached, the result can be rebirth in the brahma-plane of the first jhāna. When higher stages of jhāna are attained, the result is rebirth in higher brahma-planes in accordance with the stage of jhāna which produces rebirth. However, the highest benefit which can be reached is, after the realisation of the four noble Truths at enlightenment, to attain the state of the arahat, the perfected one. Then there will be the end of rebirth. The text states that when one does not penetrate to the highest dhamma, that is, the state of the arahat, one will be reborn in the Brahma-world. What is most important is the realisation of the noble Truths. This should be one's goal. Therefore mettā should be developed together with satipaṭṭhāna and not merely for the sake of attaining calm to the degree of access concentration or jhāna. We should develop satipaṭṭhāna time and again in our daily life, and then the other kinds of kusala will also grow.

As we read in the sutta, the Buddha also said that the person who, with mindfulness established, develops boundless mettā will realise the elimination of attachment and all other "fetters".

He will not harm any being while he develops mettā-citta, he will only be intent on what is wholesome. He has compassion for all beings, he is an excellent person with abundant merit.

7

Benefits of mettā

We read about eleven benefits of mettā in the Gradual Sayings (Book of the Elevens, Chapter II, §5, Advantages):

> Monks, eleven advantages are to be looked for from the release of heart (cetovimutti) by the practice of mettā, by making mettā to grow, by making much of it, by making mettā a vehicle and a basis, by persisting in it, by becoming familiar with it, by well establishing it. What are the eleven?
>
> One sleeps happy and wakes happy; he sees no evil dream; he is dear to human beings and non-human beings alike; the devas guard him; fire, poison or sword afflict him not; quickly he concentrates his mind; his complexion is serene; he makes an end without bewilderment; and if he has penetrated no

> further (to arahatship) he reaches (at death) the Brahma-world.
>
> These eleven advantages are to be looked for from the release of heart by the practice of mettā... by well establishing mettā.

The same eleven benefits of the development of mettā are mentioned in the Path of Discrimination (Treatise XVI, loving-kindness). The Path of Discrimination deals with the development of mettā which is fortified by the five "spiritual faculties" or indriyas (confidence, energy, sati, concentration and understanding), and the five powers, balas. The indriyas develop in satipaṭṭhāna, and they can become firm and unshakable, they can become "powers".

If one does not develop satipaṭṭhāna in one's daily life it is difficult to have true loving-kindness, because mettā needs the support of the indriyas and balas which develop in satipaṭṭhāna. To the degree that mettā is supported by these cetasikas, it becomes more established; there will be less disturbance by defilements and this means more calm. When mettā is well established it is unshakable, it does not waver because of defilements. Thus, for the development of mettā there must be a detailed knowledge of one's different cittas, there must be sati sampajañña which knows when there is wavering and when mettā is firm and unshakable. In order to know this, right understanding of one's cittas is indispensable. Defilements can only be eradicated by paññā which knows the characteristic of the reality appearing right now. Right understanding of this very moment should be developed, because what is past has gone already and the future has not come yet. Paññā which arises falls away again but because each citta which falls away is succeeded by the next one, paññā can be accumulated from moment to moment, and in this way there are conditions for paññā to become more established.

When we read about the benefits of mettā we can, instead of

wishing for these benefits, check to what extent we have developed mettā already. If we do not have these eleven benefits it is evident that we have not sufficiently developed mettā.

Question: The arahat is habitually inclined to mettā. Why did Mahā Moggallāna have to be killed through the sword?

Sujin: That was the result of past kamma. Of course, since the time he had become an arahat, he did not commit any more kamma.

Question: I would think that since he was an arahat he could not receive such a result of kamma. Past akusala kamma would be in this case "ahosi kamma", kamma which is ineffectual.

Sujin: So long as the arahat has not passed away there are still conditions for past kamma to produce result. When the arahat has finally passed away there is no more rebirth, no more arising of citta, cetasika and rūpa, and then there cannot be anymore receiving of the result of kamma.

When sati arises we can find out whether there is mettā, we can know whether it is strong or weak. Sati can be aware of the characteristic of mettā, it can find out whether there is true mettā or not. The characteristic of mettā may be confused with the characteristic of lobha. If there is no sati sampajañña it cannot be known whether there is mettā or lobha. We usually want other people to be happy, but do we want this because we love them with attachment or because we have true loving-kindness for them without any selfishness? When there is sati sampajañña we will know whether there is at such a moment lobha or mettā. When we really understand the difference mettā can develop and lobha can decrease.

People may doubt whether there is lobha or mettā when they want their parents to be happy, because lobha and mettā seem to be similar. When we think of the good qualities of our parents and we desire their welfare there is kusala citta with mettā.

When we love our parents and we are attached to them there is lobha. It is the same with the relationship of parents towards children, when they have selfish affection or possessive love for their children; there is lobha. However, if they have listened to the Dhamma and developed satipaṭṭhāna and if they can distinguish the difference between the characteristics of mettā and of lobha, they will have more mettā towards their children and less attachment. If they do not develop mettā there will be selfishness, they consider their child as "our child". Attachment to one's child can even lead to harming someone else's child. In that case there is no mettā towards one's child but selfish affection.

We read in the Visuddhimagga, in the section on the Divine Abiding of Mettā (IX, 11), that if a person wants to develop mettā he should extend it first towards someone who has moral excellence and other good qualities, someone he esteems and respects, such as his teacher. When we think of the qualities of such a person our mind becomes gentle, we have no thoughts of malevolence. We wish to help our teacher, to do everything for his benefit and happiness. Thus, the citta which thinks of the good qualities of one's teacher is gentle and mellow, it is citta with mettā. When we are happy to give assistance to someone we meet in daily life, in the same way as we would give assistance to our teacher, it is evident that we have mettā towards that person.

The Buddha praised the development of mettā, even if it is just for a short moment. We should not think that there is any kind of kusala which is unimportant, we should remember that even a short moment of kusala is beneficial. We read in the Kindred Sayings (II, Nidāna vagga, Chapter XX, Kindred Sayings on Parables, §4, The rich gift) that the Buddha, while he was staying at Sāvatthī, at the Jeta Grove, said to the monks:

> If anyone, monks, were to give a morning gift of a hundred "ukkas", and the same at noon and the

> same at eventide, or if anyone would develop mettā in the morning, at noon or at eventide, even if it were as slight as one pull at a cow's udder, this practice would be by far the more fruitful of the two.
>
> Wherefore, monks, thus should you train yourselves: liberation of heart by mettā (mettā cetovimutti) we will develop, we will often practise it, we will make it a vehicle and a base, take our stand upon it, store it up, thoroughly set it going.

The Buddha taught that all kusala dhammas can be gradually developed. Even if one finds it difficult to develop kusala, it can be accumulated so that it can arise more often and become more powerful. We should not think that we can have a great deal of mettā immediately, but each short moment of mettā is a condition that mettā develops. Otherwise the Buddha would not have taught that mettā even for the duration of one pull of a cow's udder is beneficial.

When we develop mettā we should know for what purpose we develop it. Do we develop it in order to attain calm to the degree of access-concentration or attainment-concentration? Or do we want to develop it in our daily life? Mettā and the other "perfections" are necessary conditions for the realisation of the four Noble Truths at enlightenment. We are bound to be for an endlessly long time in the cycle of birth and death, and we do not know when the perfections will have developed to the degree that enlightenment can be attained. Therefore, we should develop all kinds of kusala in order that eventually defilements can be completely eradicated and the state of the arahat can be attained. Only then will there be the end of the cycle of birth and death. Some people believe that defilements can be eradicated without the development of mettā. Or they believe that mettā is too difficult and therefore they do not develop it. They do not understand that mettā should be developed in order that it can arise again and again. Only if it arises time and again can it gradually be accumulated. We may believe that mettā is too difficult but we should remember that the arising of paññā which realises the noble Truths is even more difficult. We should not be discouraged, we should not give akusala the opportunity to gain in strength by wrongly believing that mettā is too difficult, that it cannot arise and that it therefore should not be developed. When sati arises we can have right understanding of the development of mettā: we can see that it can arise, that it can be developed little by little. In this way mettā will become more powerful, it will become steadfast. There can be mettā with our actions, our speech and our thoughts.

When we begin to develop mettā it is necessary to first see the disadvantage of dosa, aversion or anger. Dosa is the dhamma which is opposed to mettā. Whenever dosa arises it is evident that mettā is lacking. Dosa is the dhamma (reality) which is harsh, it causes harm to ourselves and to others. When dosa arises it overwhelms the citta, it inflames citta like a fire. The destructive power of dosa causes people to harm others through body and speech, in various degrees in accordance with its strength. We read in the Kindred Sayings (I, Sagāthā-vagga, I, The Devas, 8, Slaughter suttas, §1) that a deva (heavenly being) asked the Buddha:

> What must we slay if we would live happily?
> What must we slay if we would weep no more?
> What is it above all other things, whereof
> The slaughter you approve, Gotama?

The Buddha answered:

> Wrath must you slay if you would live happily,
> Wrath must you slay if you would weep no more.
> Of anger, deva, with its poisoned root

> And fevered climax which is sweet,
> That is the slaughter by the ariyans praised;
> That must you slay to weep no more.

This shows that when anger arises there is disturbance of mind, we are unhappy. We have unkind thoughts or even malevolence, we may harm the person we are angry with through body or speech so that he will suffer. We can harm him in different ways, for example by violence, by hitting him and causing him to suffer bodily injuries. Or we may utter harsh, fierce words. When we have injured someone else through body and speech we may be satisfied with what we have done. The Buddha said that wrath has a poisonous root and a sweet tip. The feeling of satisfaction we have when we have done harm to someone else is compared to the sweet tip of anger, but its root is poisoned. Each person will receive the result of his action. When dosa conditions someone to do harm to another person there is akusala kamma which has a poisonous root: akusala kamma produces an unpleasant result for the person who performs it in the form of loss and other unpleasant experiences. It can cause rebirth in unhappy planes such as a hell plane, the plane of ghosts (petas) or demons (asuras), or rebirth as an animal, depending on the degree of that akusala kamma.

If we see the disadvantage of akusala citta and akusala kamma we will develop mettā in order to diminish the accumulation of the different akusala dhammas. We should consider the benefit of patience, patience for the development of kusala and perseverance with it, so that akusala can be eliminated. We read in the Middle Length Sayings (I, no. 21, Discourse on the Parable of the Saw) that the Buddha, while staying near Sāvatthī, at the Jeta Grove, said to the monks:

> There are, monks, these five ways of speaking in which others when speaking to you might speak: at a right time or at a wrong time; according to fact or

> not according to fact; gently or harshly; on what is connected with the goal or on what is not connected with the goal; with a mind of friendliness or full of hatred. Monks, when speaking to others you might speak at a right time or at a wrong time; monks, when speaking to others you might speak according to fact or not according to fact; monks, when speaking to others you might speak about what is connected with the goal or about what is not connected with the goal; monks, when speaking to others you might speak with a mind of friendliness or full of hatred. Herein, monks, you should train yourselves thus: "Neither will our minds become perverted nor will we utter an evil speech, but kindly and compassionate will we dwell, with a mind of friendliness, void of hatred; and we will dwell having suffused that person with a mind of friendliness; and, beginning with him, we will dwell having suffused the whole world with a mind of friendliness that is far-reaching, widespread, immeasurable, without enmity, without malevolence." This is how you must train yourselves, monks.

In this sutta several similes are used to show that when there is mettā there cannot be any anguish. Mettā-citta is for example compared to a cat-skin bag which is supple and well cured. Even when someone hits it with a piece of wood no noise at all can be heard. In the same way, when there is mettā-citta, there cannot be anything which could cause the arising of dosa. We read that the Buddha said:

> Monks, as low-down thieves might carve one limb from limb with a double-handled saw, yet even then whoever sets his mind at enmity, he, for this reason, is not a doer of my teaching...

8
The blessings of mettā

The Buddha taught Dhamma to his followers out of compassion, he taught them Dhamma for their benefit and happiness. When they had listened to the Dhamma they could ponder over it and develop it in daily life. The Buddha taught about the ill effects of anger. Anger leads to different kinds of suffering for the person who is angry, but the person to whom anger is directed does not have to suffer from it if he does not have anger himself. We read in the Gradual Sayings (Book of Sevens, Chapter VI, §10.) about the effects of anger. The person who is angry looks ugly. Even though he bathes himself, anoints himself, trims his hair and beard and dresses himself in clean, white linen, for all that he is ugly, since he is overwhelmed by anger. When someone is angry his face is tense, and sometimes his mouth may be distorted and his speech blurred. He may lie on a couch spread with a fleecy cover, a white blanket, a woollen coverlet, flower-embroidered, with crimson cushions, but for all that, if he is overwhelmed by anger, he lies in discomfort. He may know what is good and what is evil, but when he is overwhelmed by anger he does what is harmful, not what is beneficial. When one performs unwholesome deeds through body, speech and mind, one will have as result an unhappy rebirth in lower planes, such as a hell plane or the animal world, depending on the kamma which produces rebirth.

We read in the Gradual Sayings (Book of the Sevens, Chapter VI, §10. Anger), that the Buddha said:

> How ugly is an angry man! His sleep
> Is comfortless; with fortune in his hands
> He suffers loss; and being full of wrath
> He wounds by act and bitter word. Overwhelmed
> By rage, his wealth he wastes away. Made mad
> And crazy by his bile, his name's bemired.
> With odium, shunned and forsaken is
> An angry man by friend and relative.
> By wrath is loss incurred; by wrath, the mind
> Irate, he knows not that within
> Fear is engendered, nor knows the goal.
> When anger-bound, man Dhamma cannot see;
> When anger conquers man, blind darkness reigns.
> A man in wrath finds pleasure in bad deeds,
> As in good deeds; yet later when his wrath
> Is spent, he suffers like one scorched by fire:
> As flame atop of smoke, he staggers on,
> When anger spreads, when youth becomes incensed.
> No shame, no fear of blame, no reverence
> In speech has he whose mind is anger rent;
> No island of support he ever finds.
> The deeds which bring remorse, far from right states,

These I'll proclaim. Listen how they come about.
A man in anger will his father kill,
In wrath his very mother will he slay,
Arahats and ordinary men alike he will kill.
By his mother's care man sees the light
Of day, yet common average folk, in wrath,
Will still destroy that fount of life.
Self-mirrored all these beings are; each one
Loves self most. In wrath the ordinary men
Kill self, by divers forms distraught: by sword
Men kill themselves; in madness poison take;
And in some hollow of a mountain glen
They hide, and bind themselves with ropes and die.
Thus ruin runs in wake of wrath, and they
Who act in wrath, perceive not that their deeds,
Destroying life, bring death for themselves.
Thus lurking in the heart is Māra's snare
In anger's loathsome form. But root it out
By insight, zeal, right view, restraint; the wise
Would one by one eradicate each akusala,
And thus in Dhamma would he train himself:
Be not our minds obscured, but anger freed
And freed from trouble, greed and envy.
The well trained, the canker-freed. Become,
When anger is stilled, wholly, completely cool.

Question: I find what I heard about mettā very beneficial. However, mettā does not arise whenever I wish in the situations of daily life. What should I do in order that mettā can arise?

Sujin: When someone takes realities for self he is inclined to believe that there is a self who can, by following a particular method, suppress dosa and develop sati and mettā. However, in reality there isn't anybody who can have sati and mettā if there are no conditions for their arising. Listening to the Dhamma, wisely considering what one heard, intellectual understanding of the Dhamma are different moments of kusala. They are accumulated from moment to moment, and together they make up conditions for the arising of sati later on which is mindful of one's different cittas. In this way the disadvantage of dosa and the benefit of mettā can be seen. However, if sati does not arise and there are conditions for dosa, dosa will arise. There is nobody who can have sati and kindness at will. If sati arises and it can, time and again, be mindful of the Dhamma which the Buddha explained, there are conditions for the elimination of anger. If one does not often listen to the Dhamma there are not many conditions for wise consideration of it and then it is difficult to subdue dosa. Whereas if one listens a great deal there are conditions for remembrance and wise consideration of the Dhamma. One may for example reflect on kamma and its result. People are the owners of their deeds. There can be wise consideration of akusala kamma which is motivated by anger, it can be remembered that anger is not helpful for the attainment of enlightenment. People can reflect on the development of patience by the Buddha during his lives as a Bodhisatta, as it is described in the "Sīlavanāga Jātaka" (I, 72), the "Khantivādi Jātaka" (III, 313), the "Culladhammapāla Jātaka" (III, 358), or the "Chaddanta Jātaka" (V, 514). They can apply what they read in the Buddha's teachings. The Buddha taught the Dhamma out of compassion to his followers so that they would carefully consider it and develop it in daily life.

I will quote from the "Mahā-mangala Jātaka" (IV, 453) in order that the meaning of "mangala", auspicious sign or blessing, will be clearer. Everybody desires blessings, things which are auspicious. Sometimes people search for it, they believe that they have a mangala if they possess a particular thing or if they recite particular texts. We should know what a real mangala is. We read in the "Mahā-mangala Jātaka" that mettā is a mangala.

When we know that, we will not search for something else. A true mangala is the citta with mettā, mettā through body, speech and mind. When the citta is kusala, the citta is beautiful, it is "auspicious".

We read in the "Mahā-mangala Jātaka" that people asked the Bodhisatta, when he was a hermit, what a mangala is which gives blessings in this world and the next. We read that the Bodhisatta explained:

> Whoso the devas, and all the brahmas,
> And reptiles, and all beings, which we see,
> Honours forever with a kindly heart,
> The wise call this a mangala.
>
> Who is humble towards all beings
> To men, women and children alike,
> Who to reviling does not answer back,
> His patience the wise call a mangala.
>
> Who is of clear understanding, in crisis wise,
> Nor playmates nor companions does despise,
> Nor boasts of birth, wisdom, caste or wealth,
> The wise call this a mangala for his friends.
>
> Who takes good men and true his friends to be,
> Who trust him, for his tongue from venom free,
> Who never harms a friend, who shares his wealth,
> The wise call this a mangala for his friends.
>
> Whose wife is friendly and of equal years,
> Devoted, good, and many children bears,
> Faithful, virtuous, and of gentle birth.
> The wise call that a mangala in wives.

Whose King the mighty Lord of beings is,
Who has purity of sīla, is diligent,
And says, "He is my friend", and means no guile,
That the wise call a mangala in Kings.

Who has confidence, gives food and drink,
Flowers, garlands and perfumes,
With heart at peace, and spreading joy around,
This the wise call a mangala in heavenly planes.

Whom by good living virtuous sages try
With effort strenuous to purify,
Good men and wise, by tranquil life built up,
The wise call this a mangala among the company of
arahats.

These blessings then, that in the world befall,
Esteemed by all the wise,
Which man is prudent let him follow these,
The omens which are seen, heard or touched are not
real.

Some people believe that when they see something special such as a red cow there is a mangala, that it brings them luck. Others believe that when they hear a special sound or words by which good wishes are conveyed to them, there is a mangala which is heard. Others again believe that when they touch particular things, such as a white dress or a white headgear, or when they apply white powder, there is a mangala by touch. Or when they smell a particular flower, or taste a special flavour they believe that there is a mangala through the senses of smell or taste. As we have read in the Jātaka, there is no truth in such omens experienced through the senses, they are based on superstition. Mettā is a real mangala.

Question: Can one extend mettā to devas (heavenly beings)?

Sujin: In respect to this, people should carefully consider which cause brings which effect. In which way do we extend mettā to devas? In the human plane mettā can be developed by dāna, by giving other people useful things, or by sīla, by abstaining from harming others, by abstaining from anger and malevolence. As regards developing mettā towards devas, the situation is different. Birth as a deva is produced by kusala kamma and the lifespan of devas is extremely long. Its length depends on the degree of kusala kamma which produced birth in that plane. Therefore we cannot extend mettā to devas by abstaining from killing them or by abstaining from other kinds of akusala kamma which could harm them. We can think with appreciation of their good deeds which conditioned birth as a deva, thus, there can be "anumodhana dāna". Or when we do good deeds we can extend merit to the devas so that they can have anumodhana dāna, kusala cittas with appreciation. These are ways of extending mettā to devas.

Question: I do not understand yet how we can extend merit to devas when we perform dāna or other kinds of kusala.

Sujin: When we perform a good deed devas can appreciate such a deed. However, one should not hope for their protection just by reciting texts. When we have expectations there is lobha and that is different from performing kusala and extending merit so that devas can appreciate one's kusala and also have kusala cittas.

Question: Thus, we can extend merit to devas?

Sujin: Yes, when we perform kusala we can extend merit to devas. However, human beings cannot give things such as food to devas, because devas take a different kind of food, more refined than our food. Devas have great wealth, they have precious stones such as diamonds and sapphires, they have valuable jewellery, they have more riches than any king in the world. This is due to their great merit which caused them to be born as devas.

As a human being one cannot offer them anything, one can only extend merit to them when one does good deeds.

Someone may wish to extend mettā to devas by reciting texts on mettā, and he may expect that they will protect him. However, when he, inspite of this, meets misfortune and trouble, and thus his expectations about being protected by the devas do not come true, he will be disappointed and he may blame the devas. Whereas when the citta has true calm and it is only intent on kusala, there is no expectation of any result, and thus people will not blame anyone, there will be no disappointment or unhappiness.

Question: In Thailand there is the belief that one should pay respect to guardian spirits and brahmas. Do they really exist and can they assist us?

Sujin: First of all we should consider whether there is birth in other planes of existence, such as the deva planes, and whether there are beings in other planes such as guardian spirits and brahmas. There is birth in planes other than the human plane, depending on the appropriate conditions. Birth as a deva is the result of kusala kamma and this kind of birth is higher than birth as a human being. Birth in a brahma plane is the result of jhāna. If samatha has been developed to the degree of jhāna and the jhānacitta does not decline but arises shortly before the dying-consciousness, it produces rebirth-consciousness in a brahma plane. Thus beings who are brahmas really exist.

Some people believe that there are sacred shrines or other objects they should venerate, but why do they attach importance to such things? We should remember that everybody is the owner of the deeds he has performed himself. Kamma conditions people to have different pleasant or unpleasant experiences in life. We see, hear, smell, taste and experience through body-sense different objects, some pleasant, some unpleasant. Seeing, hearing, smelling, tasting and the experience of tangible object are cittas which are results of kamma, vipākacittas. If there were no kammas which have been performed and which are capable of producing vipāka, all those different experiences could not arise.

As to the question about the assistance to people given by guardian spirits and brahmas, each person is "heir" to his own deeds; that means: pleasant and unpleasant experiences through the senses are produced accordingly by the kamma he performed. Someone told me about an event which happened. When he was driving his car with a little boy sitting beside him, his car slipped off the road. However, the driver of a jeep who was immediately behind him stopped and could help him to get the car back on the road again, because he had the right equipment with him. The driver of the car who had this experience understood that if there had been conditions for akusala kamma to produce akusala vipāka (unpleasant result), he would not have received help so soon and in that case he would have had to wait much longer to get his car back on the road. We may receive help from another person, be he human or non-human, but this also depends on kamma. If there are conditions for akusala kamma to produce result, neither human being nor non-human being can help us. From the example given above we see that accumulated kusala kamma is like a close friend who is near and who can give protection and assistance, who can solve problems in different situations.

9

Cause and result in life

Some people may worship Brahmas but they do not know where they are, how one can be born as a Brahma and what life as a Brahma is like. We read in the Kindred Sayings (I, Sagāthā-vagga, Chapter VI, The Brahmā Suttas, §3, Brahmadeva) that people worshipped Brahma already during the Buddha's time. The text states:

> Thus have I heard: The Exalted One was once staying at Sāvatthī, in the Jeta Grove, in Anāthapiṇḍaka's Park.
>
> Now on that occasion Brahmadeva, son of a certain brahminee, left the world, going from home into the homeless in the Order of the Exalted One. And the venerable Brahmadeva, remaining alone and separate, earnest, ardent, and strenuous, attained ere

long to that supreme goal of the higher life, for the sake of which the clansmen rightly go forth from home into the homeless; that supreme goal did he by himself, even in this present life, come to understand and realise. He came to understand that birth was destroyed, that the holy life was being lived, that his task was done, that for life as we conceive it, there was no hereafter. And the venerable Brahmadeva thus became one of the arahats.

Now the venerable Brahmadeva rose early one morning, and dressing himself, took robe and bowl and entered Sāvatthī for alms. And going about Sāvatthī, house by house, he came to his mother's dwelling.

At that time his mother, the brahminee, was habitually making an oblation to Brahmā. Then it occurred to Brahmā Sahampati: "This mother of the venerable Brahmadeva, the brahminee, makes her perpetual oblation to Brahmā. What if I were now to approach and agitate her?" So as a strong man might stretch forth his bent arm, or bend his arm stretched forth, Brahmā Sahampati vanished from the Brahmā world and appeared at the dwelling of the mother of the venerable Brahmadeva. And standing in the air he addressed her in verses:

Far from here, O brahminee, is Brahma's world,
To whom you always serve offerings.
And Brahmā does not take food like that.
What babble you unwitting of the way,
O brahminee, unto the Brahma world.
Look at Brahmadeva, your son,
A man who will never see another world,
A man who past the gods has won his way,

An almsman who does nothing call his own,
Who only maintains himself,
This man has come into your house for alms,
Worthy of offerings, versed in the Vedas,
With faculties developed and controlled.
It is suitable for devas and men to offer to him
True brahmin, barring all things evil out,
By evil undefiled, grown calm and cool,
He moves on his alms round.
There is no after, no before for him,
He is at peace, no fume of vice is his;
He is untroubled, rid of hankering;
All force renouncing toward both weak and strong.
Let him enjoy the choice food you have served.
By all the hosts of evil unassailed,
His heart at utter peace, he goes about
Like tamed elephant, with vices purged.
Almsman most virtuous, and with heart well freed:
Let him enjoy the choice food you have served.
To him so worthy of the gift do you,
In confidence unwavering, offer your gift.
Work merit and your future happiness,
Now that you see here, O brahminee,
A sage by whom the flood is overpassed.
To him so worthy of the gift did she,
In confidence unwavering, offer her gift.
Merit she wrought, her future happiness,
When (at her door) the brahminee saw
A sage by whom the flood was overpassed.

Should one make an offering to an arahat or to Brahmā? When one has right understanding one will know that it is better to make an offering to an arahat who has eradicated all defilements. He has accomplished the task which has to be done and there is nothing more to be done by him since all defilements have been completely eradicated. Although the son of the brahminee had attained arahatship, the brahminee still paid respect to Brahmā and she made continuously offerings of food to him. The brahma planes are far away from the human plane, the distance to those planes is immeasurable. Brahmas cannot eat food offered by humans. The Brahminee did not know how the brahma world could be reached, but she offered food to Brahmā and in her ignorance she mumbled words to him over and over again.

The Sāratthappakāsinī, the Commentary to the Kindred Sayings, gives an elaboration of the story about the Brahminee.

> When the mother of Brahmadeva had seen her son approaching her house, she went outside to welcome him. She invited him to come inside and to sit on a seat she had prepared. It was her custom to offer rice cakes to Brahmā and also on that day she performed sacrificial worship. Her whole house was decorated with fresh green leaves and puffed rice, with precious stones and flowers. She had put up different kinds of flags and banners and she had laid out water vessels. She had lighted candles contained in candle holders which were decorated with garlands and many fragrant things. People went around in procession. The brahminee herself had got up very early in the morning. After she had bathed herself with fragrant water taken from sixteen pots, she put on beautiful cloths and precious jewellery. She invited her son, the arahat, to come inside, but she had no intention to offer him even a ladle of rice. She only wanted to attend to Mahā Brahmā, to make sacrificial worship to him. She filled a golden tray with rice, prepared with ghee, honey and sugar. She

carried the tray to the backyard which she had decorated with fresh green leaves. She had put a lump of rice on each of the four corners of the tray and took one lump at a time in her hand while the ghee was dripping on her arms. She knelt down on the ground and recited an invitation to Mahā Brahmā to partake of the food.

In the meantime Brahmā Sahampati inhaled the fragrance of the sīla of the arahat which rose to all deva planes and was diffused even as far as the brahma planes. The odours of the human world do not reach the brahma planes, it is only the fragrance of the excellent qualities of arahats which can be diffused as far as that. It occurred to Sahampati that he should admonish the brahminee and explain to her what would be the right thing for her to do. He said to her: "You have not even given a ladle of rice to your son after he sat down, although he is most worthy of offerings. Instead you have only thought of offering food to Mahā Brahmā. The situation is the same as when someone who has scales for weighing discards them and just uses his hands, or someone who has a drum does not make use of it but beats on his stomach instead, or someone who has a fire does not make use of it but uses a firefly instead."

Sahampati wanted to induce her to change her mind, to offer food to her son the arahat instead of offering it to Mahā Brahmā.

He said to himself: "I will cause her wrong view to disappear and save her from an unhappy plane. I will convert her to the Buddha's teachings so that she will accumulate an immeasurable treasure, namely kusala kamma which will produce as result rebirth in a heavenly plane."

The distance from here to the brahma planes is difficult to fathom. If a stone which has the size of a tall building would travel from the lowest brahma plane as fast as 48.000 yoyanas (one yoyana being 16 km.) a day, it would take four months before it would reach the earth. The lowest brahma plane is as far as that, and the higher planes are still further away.

Sahampati said: "Very far indeed is the world of Brahmā, to whom you, Brahminee, are making the offering of food. The real way to attain to the world of Brahmā are the kusala jhānacittas of the four stages of jhāna. These give as results the four types of vipāka jhānacittas which arise in the brahma planes. You do not know the way to attain the world of Brahmā, you are only mumbling some prayers. Those who are in brahma planes keep alive by jhāna rapture and not by taking rice or drinking boiled milk. You should not trouble yourself with things which are not the real condition for the attainment to the world of Brahmā."

When Sahampati had spoken thus and respectfully took leave of the Brahminee, he pointed to the arahat and spoke again:

"Brahminee, your son Brahmadeva has eradicated all defilements, he is the highest among devas, the highest among Brahmas. He is no more disturbed by defilements. He is an almsman who has the habit of asking, who does not provide a livelihood for someone else. The great Brahmadeva who entered your house for alms is the person who is most worthy to receive an offering of food."

This is the story related by the Commentary. In order to be

reborn as a Brahma in a Brahma plane there must be the right condition. One should develop samatha to the stage of jhāna, which can be rūpa-jhāna or arūpa-jhāna. This is the way to rūpa-brahma planes and arūpa-brahma planes. The result of kusala jhānacitta is rebirth in a brahma plane where one will live until the jhāna kusala kamma has been exhausted and one will pass away from that plane. Beings in brahma planes do not need to eat and they do not need to breathe in order to stay alive. Beings in the rūpa-brahma planes have very subtle rūpas and these do not have to be sustained by morsels of food such as is taken by human beings, and they do not have to experience suffering due to breathing. As regards beings in the arūpa-brahma planes, they do not have any rūpa.

As the Commentary states, Brahmadeva had eradicated all defilements, he was the highest among devas. The arahat who is not disturbed by defilements does not have to provide a livelihood for someone else. When one hears this one thinks of the bhikkhus who do not have a family and who do not have a profession by which they have to provide a livelihood for others. However, there is a deeper meaning to these words. The meaning is that for the arahat there are no more conditions for rebirth, for the arising of khandhas in a future life. So long as one still has defilements, there will be a new life after this one, conditioned by these defilements. When at the end of life the dying-consciousness has fallen away there will be rebirth, there will be nāma khandhas and rūpa khandhas succeeding the khandhas which are arising and falling away in this life, which we take for "I" or "mine", for "my personality". Our present life conditions the life of a future being, of someone else, namely the khandhas arising in the future which are conditioned by the khandhas in this life. In this sense it is said that we maintain or sustain the life of someone else.

The Brahmadeva Sutta can answer the questions about spirits and brahmas who are venerated in Thailand, questions about whether they exist and whether they can help us.

Question: I believe that there is someone who is an avenger, who can cause us to suffer misfortune. When we do good deeds and then transfer the merit to this person can that be to our benefit? When one develops samādhi can one then see such a person?

Sujin: The Buddha taught about cause and effect and we should carefully consider this. Is it true that there is someone who could inflict retribution on us and thus control our fate? We read in the Gradual Sayings (Book of the Tens, Chapter XXI, §6) that the Buddha taught to the monks about kamma and its result:

> Monks, beings are owners of their deeds, heirs to their deeds, they are the womb of their deeds, their deeds are their relatives, to them their deeds come home again. Whatsoever deeds they do, be they good or evil, of these deeds they are the heirs.

When someone is born as this person into this world, what is the cause? Is this caused by the kamma he performed himself or by someone else who controls his fate?

When a person has gain, honour, praise, happiness, or when he has loss, dishonour, blame and misery, by what are these caused? Are they caused by someone else who controls his fate or are they results of deeds he has performed himself?

People believe that someone to whom they in former lives caused suffering can have power over their fate, that he follows them in this life and causes them to be ill or to suffer different kinds of misfortunes. Or if such a person has not caused their misfortune yet, they believe that they should extend merit to him so that he will not cause them to suffer.

Who can remember his former lives and the deeds he performed during those lives? Who can remember to which being he caused trouble and suffering in past lives? If someone, for example, has killed another person and then extends merit to him how could this prevent the killing which is akusala kamma from producing result? One should know who the owner is of the kammas which have been performed during the cycle of birth and death. Akusala kamma such as killing can cause rebirth in a hell plane. Or if one is born in the human plane akusala kamma can cause one to be sick or to suffer misfortune. Kusala kamma can cause rebirth in a happy plane, such as rebirth as a human being, or as a deva in one of the heavenly planes. Rebirth is in accordance with the kamma one performed oneself. If there is an unhappy rebirth it is not due to any revenge of another being. There is no one who could rule over someone's destiny.

If people believe in a person who could retaliate, how is their relationship to such a person? If they think that there is a person who could take revenge then they themselves could also be someone who takes revenge on another person. However, when someone has no ill feeling towards others could he take revenge and cause someone else's misfortune? We may remember ill deeds in this life which we have committed to someone else and ill deeds which others have committed to us, but we do not remember the deeds which were committed in past lives. We would not be able to remember to whom we did wrong ourselves, nor would others be able to remember such things. Thus the belief in someone who could take revenge for the wrongs a person formerly did to him and who could cause his misfortune in this life is without foundation. The transfer of merit to such a person is also useless, it does not have any effect.

Every being has performed many kammas during countless aeons in the past. People are born and they must die, they are born again and must die again, and thus they are now no longer the same person they were in the past. We should not think of a person in the past who could take revenge, but instead we should remember that in this life one should have no anger, no revengeful feeling, no wish to harm or hurt anyone. People may have aversion or anger or they may even want to hurt someone else when they think that he in this life or in a former life caused them misfortune or suffering. However, one should subdue one's anger and feelings of revenge and not commit any deed motivated by anger. Instead, one should develop mettā and make it increase.

10

Mettā: foundation of the world

The Buddha said that beings are owners of their deeds, heirs to their deeds, that kamma is the womb from which they are born, that their deeds are their relatives. To them their deeds come home again and whatsoever deeds they do, be they good or evil, of those deeds they receive the results.

Everybody is the owner of his deeds, he possesses the kamma he has performed. People cannot exchange their kammas. Other kinds of possessions do not really belong to us, they can be destroyed or stolen. The kamma we have performed ourselves, be it kusala kamma or akusala kamma, cannot be stolen or damaged by fire, wind or sun. There is no possession which can be kept as safely as kamma, because kamma is accumulated from moment to moment, since cittas arise and fall away in succession.

When kamma has been performed it can cause the arising of

vipāka (result) for the person who committed it, if there are the right conditions for kamma to produce result. The person who has performed kamma will receive its result accordingly, since kamma is the "womb", it can condition rebirth in a happy plane or in an unhappy plane. When we are born, kamma is a "relative" (kinsman) to us, we are dependant on our kamma. When there are conditions for akusala kamma to produce its result, then akusala kamma is our "relative": there is the arising of unpleasant experiences and misfortunes, of which the immediate occasion can even be our circle of relatives and friends, or other people we are acquainted with. When kusala kamma has the opportunity to produce its result, the opposite happens, and thus we can say that each person has kamma as his relative, that he is dependant on his kamma.

When we experience happiness or misery on account of visible object, sound, odour, flavour and tangible object, it seems that other people are the cause of such experiences. When we for example have been hurt or harmed by others, it seems that other people are the cause of this. However, could this really happen if there were no akusala kamma we performed ourselves which produces such result? When akusala kamma has the opportunity to produce result we will receive its result, even if there are no people around who could hurt us. We may, for example, wound ourselves with a knife, we may fall down, we may become ill, we may suffer from an inundation or a fire. Some people may believe that there is another person who could avenge himself and cause them to suffer from sickness and other misfortunes. They extend merit to that person out of fear of his retaliation. However, all this is a superstition.

When we have performed kusala kamma we can extend merit to others who are able to appreciate our good deed, and this is a form of dāna, of generosity. It is beneficial to do this, because at such a moment the citta is accompanied by mettā. We think of the well-being of someone else, we give him the opportunity to have kusala citta with appreciation of our kusala. When somebody has "anumodhana dāna", appreciation of another person's kusala, it is his kusala kamma. We all can rejoice in each others kusala, by anumodhana dāna, and in this way benefit from the good deeds performed by someone else. However, we should not extend merit out of fear that there is someone who could avenge himself and cause misfortune. The development of mettā towards those we meet in this life is more beneficial than the extension of merit to an avenger we have never seen and whom we do not know.

We read in the Commentary to the Dhammapada (vs. 136) that the Buddha told the bhikkhus a story of the past, which happened at the time of Buddha Kassapa. The treasurer Sumangala had a Vihāra built for the Buddha Kassapa. One day when Sumangala was on his way to the Teacher, he saw a robber, hidden in a rest house at the gate of the city, his feet spattered with mud, a robe drawn over his head. Sumangala said to himself: "This man must be a night-prowler in hiding". Then that robber conceived a grudge against Sumangala. He burned his field seven times, cut off the feet of his cattle seven times and burned his house seven times. However, he had not satisfied his grudge yet against the treasurer. When he found out that Sumangala rejoiced most of all in the Buddha's Perfumed Chamber, he destroyed that by fire. When Sumangala saw the Perfumed Chamber destroyed by fire he did not have the slightest grief but he clapped his hands with joy since he would be once more permitted to built a Perfumed Chamber for the Buddha. He rebuilt the Perfumed Chamber and presented it to the Buddha and his retinue of twenty thousand monks. When the robber saw that, he decided to kill Sumangala. He took a knife and went around the monastery for seven days. During these days Sumangala made gifts to the Sangha presided over by the Buddha. He told the Buddha what had happened and said that he would transfer to that man the first fruits of the merit of his offering. When the robber heard this he realised that he had committed a grievous sin towards the treasurer who had no ill-will and even extended merit to him. He asked the treasurer forgiveness. When the treasurer asked the robber about each particular deed whether he had committed it, the robber answered him that he had committed all of them, and he explained the reason. He said that he had conceived a grudge against the treasurer when he had heard his words while he was lying down splattered with mud near the city gate. Sumangala asked him for forgiveness for the words he had spoken then. The robber wanted to become the treasurer's slave and live in his house, but Sumangala declined that, since he could not be sure whether the robber would continue to have a grudge against him. Although Sumangala had forgiven the robber, the akusala kamma the robber had committed caused him to be reborn in the Avīci Hell. After he had suffered there for a long time he was reborn as a peta (ghost) on Vultures Peak in the era of this Buddha.

The treasurer had no feelings of revenge against the robber who had a grudge against him, but he had mettā towards him. He extended merit to the robber who had committed very heavy akusala kamma so that he would have kusala citta while rejoicing in Sumangala's good deeds. If Sumangala had been angry with the robber and had feelings of revenge, he himself could have received the result of his anger and of the deeds motivated by revenge.

If one is afraid of revenge one should abstain from the five kinds of akusala kamma which cause a fivefold guilty dread, namely: killing, stealing, sexual misconduct, lying and the taking of intoxicants. One should abstain from these akusala kammas. The Buddha said that people who only fear those things which should be feared are no fools, whereas people who only fear what should not be feared are fools. Those who develop an understanding of the Dhamma should fear the committing of akusala kamma, they should not be afraid of a person who could take revenge and control their destiny.

Someone asked whether one, if one develops samādhi (concentration), could see an image of the person who wants to take revenge. There are misunderstandings about the development of samādhi, and therefore I will explain what it is. There are two kinds of samādhi, namely sammā-samādhi, right concentration, and micchā-samādhi, wrong concentration. There is sammā-samādhi with the development of samatha, tranquil meditation. This is the development of kusala citta which is established in wholesome calm so that there is more and more freedom from lobha, attachment, dosa, aversion, and moha, ignorance. Thus in samatha there must be kusala citta with sati sampajañña, paññā arising with sati, which is mindful time and again of the dhammas (realities) which condition the citta to be free from akusala and to attain true calm. Calm can be developed with meditation subjects such as the excellent qualities of the Buddha, the Dhamma and the Sangha. Or one can think of other people with mettā, karuṇā (compassion), muditā (sympathetic joy) and upekkhā (equanimity). One can recollect dāna (generosity) and sīla (good moral conduct) one has performed, or one can recollect death. When the citta has advanced in kusala it becomes more established in calm, in freedom from akusala. Then the characteristic of calm which goes together with concentration, samādhi, appears more clearly. Calm can become firmer when sati sampajañña performs its function, and this has nothing to do with the seeing of extraordinary things or strange experiences.

When calm has been developed with a meditation subject and calm has become more established, one can experience an image, nimitta, but this is not the case with all meditation subjects. The development of the following meditation subjects is dependant on the experience of a nimitta: the kasinas (disks), the meditations on corpses, mindfulness of breath (ānāpāna sati) and mindfulness with regard to the body (kāyagatā sati).

When someone develops the earth kasina he contemplates earth in order that the citta becomes calm, free of akusala; he is dependant on an image in the form of a circle, which can help him to subdue akusala citta. When someone develops the other kasinas, namely the kasinas of fire and wind, of the colours of blue, yellow, red and white, of light and air, the same procedure is followed.

The meditations on foulness (asubha) are meditations on corpses in different stages of decay.

As regards mindfulness of breath (ānāpāna sati), this is mindfulness of breath where it appears on the tip of the nose or upper lip.

Kāyagatā sati is contemplation of the foulness of the body in each part, such as hair of the head, hair of the body, nails, teeth, skin.

One is dependant on a nimitta, a mental image, only when one develops calm with the above mentioned meditation subjects. Of each of these subjects a mental image can appear. Citta contemplates this image in order to attain a higher degree of calm. Citta contemplates a specific nimitta in the case of each of these subjects and it does not "see" other nimittas such as hells, heavens, devas, ghosts or the person one calls the avenger or controller of one's fate.

The development of samatha and the development of vipassanā are intricate and difficult. For both ways of development paññā is needed but paññā in samatha and paññā in vipassanā are of different levels. Paññā in samatha can temporarily subdue defilements but it cannot eradicate them. In vipassanā paññā, is developed which knows the reality which appears as it is, as anattā, non-self, and this kind of paññā can eradicate defilements completely. People should not mistakenly think that they develop samatha or vipassanā by way of concentration, by trying to focus for a long time on one object.

If someone tries to concentrate with the expectation to see

special things he concentrates with lobha. This is not the development of true calm which is freedom from lobha, dosa and moha. He does not develop calm, because there is lobha, not paññā. There is no sati sampajañña which knows how citta can become calm, free from defilements. Sati sampajañña knows correctly how citta should contemplate a particular meditation subject in order to attain true calm. When there is no right understanding of the development of calm and one concentrates in order to have special experiences or to see extraordinary things, there is no sammā-samādhi, right concentration, but micchā-samādhi, wrong concentration. When there is micchā-samādhi, the citta is akusala, there is citta with attachment. There is clinging, one wants to concentrate, to focus for a long time on one object. When there is micchā-samādhi different mental images may appear because citta thinks of them without realizing that there is only thinking. It is the same situation as when people are dreaming, and they do not realise that the images in their dream appear only because they are thinking of them. When there is micchā-samādhi and someone sees an image he takes for the controller of his fate or an avenger, it is only a thought, an imagination, it is not right understanding which clearly realises what is true. The Buddha said that in the cycle of birth and death which is endlessly long we all were related to each other as family members, friends, husband and wife, parents and children, or as enemies. Even Devadatta, who tried to kill the Buddha, was in a former life his father. People should not extend merit to a person who could revenge himself because of a bad deed they did towards him, to a person they do not even know, since people cannot remember which bad deeds they committed to one another. Instead, we should from now on develop mettā towards each being, each person we meet in this life, in order to subdue the inclination to commit evil deeds. When people lack mettā there will be suffering. The Buddha said that mettā is the dhamma which is the foundation of the world, it is kusala dhamma which supports beings in the world so that they can live free from danger, free from the sorrow resulting from akusala citta which is without mettā.

11

Selected texts

Mettā Sutta: Sutta-Nippāta (143-152)

This is what is to be done by one who is skilful in respect of the good, having attained the peaceful state. He should be capable, straight, and very upright, easy to speak, to gentle and not proud, contented and easy to support, having few duties and of a frugal way of life, with his sense-faculties calmed, zealous, not impudent, (and) not greedy (when begging) among families.

And he should not do any mean thing, on account of which other wise men would criticise him. Let all creatures indeed be happy (and) secure; let them be happy minded.

Whatever living creatures there are, moving or still without exception, whichever are long or large, or middle-sized or short, small or great, whichever are seen or unseen, whichever live far or near, whether they already exist or are going to be, let all creatures be happy minded.

One man should not humiliate another; one should not despise anyone anywhere. One should not wish another misery because of anger or from the notion of repugnance.

Just as a mother would protect with her life her own son, her only son, so one should cultivate an unbounded mind towards all beings, and loving-kindness towards all the world. One should cultivate an unbounded mind, above and below and across, without obstruction, without enmity, without rivalry.

Standing, or going, or seated, or lying down, as long as one is free from drowsiness, one should practise this mindfulness. This, they say, is the holy state here.

Not subscribing to wrong views, virtuous, endowed with insight, having overcome greed for sensual pleasures, a creature assuredly does not come to lie again in a womb.

Sigālovāda Suttanta: Dīgha Nikāya, III, 180

Thus have I heard: The Exalted One was once staying near Rājagaha in the Bamboo Wood at the Squirrels' Feeding ground.

Now at this time young Sigāla, a householder's son, rising betimes, went forth from Rājagaha, and with wet hair and wet garments and clasped hands uplifted, paid worship to the several quarters of the earth and sky–to the east, south, west, and north, to the nadir and the zenith.

And the Exalted One, early that morning dressed himself, took bowl and robe and entered Rājagaha seeking alms. Now he saw young Sigāla worshipping and spoke to him thus:

"Why, young householder, do you, rising betimes and leaving Rājagaha, with wet hair and raiment, worship the several quarters of earth and sky?"

"Sir, my father, when he was a-dying, said to me: Dear son, you should worship the quarters of the earth and sky. So I, sir, honouring my father's word, reverencing, revering, holding it sacred, rise betimes and, leaving Rājagaha, worship on this wise."

"But in the religion of an Ariyan, young householder, the six quarters should not be worshipped thus."

"How then, sir, in the religion of an Ariyan, should the six quarters be worshipped?

It would be an excellent thing, sir, if the Exalted One would so teach me the doctrine according to which, in the religion of an Ariyan, the six quarters should be worshipped."

"Hear then, young householder, give ear to my words and I will speak.

So be it, sir, responded young Sigāla. And the Exalted One said:

"Inasmuch, young householder, as the ariyan disciple has put away the four vices in conduct, inasmuch as he does no evil actions from the four motives, inasmuch as he does not pursue the six channels for dissipating wealth, he thus, avoiding these fourteen evil things, is a coverer of the six quarters; he has practised so as to conquer both worlds; he tastes success both in this world and the next. At the dissolution of the body, after death he is reborn to a happy destiny heaven. What are the four vices of conduct that he has put away? The destruction of life, the taking what is not given, licentiousness, and lying speech. These are the four vices of conduct that he has put away."

Thus spoke the Exalted One. And when the blessed One had thus spoken, the master sake again:

"Slaughter of life, theft, lying, adultery
To these no word of praise the wise award."

"By which four motives does he do no evil deed? Evil deeds are done from motives of partiality, enmity, stupidity and fear. But inasmuch as the Ariyan disciple is not led away by these motives, he through them does no evil deed."

Thus sake Exalted One. And when the Blessed One had thus spoken, the Master sake yet again:

"Whoso from partiality or hate
Or fear or dullness doth transgress the Norm,
All minished good name and fame become
As in the ebbing month the waning moon.
Who ne'er from partiality or hate
Or fear or dullness doth transgress the Norm,
Perfect and full good name and fame become.
As in the brighter half the waxing moon."

"And which are the six channels for dissipating wealth? The being addicted to intoxicating liquors, frequenting the streets at unseemly hours, haunting fairs, the being infatuated by gambling, associating with evil companions, the habit of idleness.

"There are, young householder, these six dangers through being addicted to intoxicating liquors: actual loss of wealth, increase of quarrels, susceptibility to disease, loss of good character, indecent exposure, impaired intelligence.

"Six, young householder, are the perils from frequenting the streets at unseemly hours–he himself is without guard or protection and so also are wife and children; so also is his property; he moreover becomes suspected [as the doer] of [undiscovered] crimes, and false rumours fix on him, and many are the troubles he goes out to meet.

Six, young householder, are the perils from haunting fairs: [he is ever thinking] where is there dancing? where is there singing? where is there music? where is recitation? where are the cymbals? where the tam-tams?

"Six, young householder, are the perils for him who is infatuated with gambling: as winner he begets hatred; when beaten he mourns his lost wealth; his actual substance is wasted; his word has no weight in a court of law; he is despised by friends and officials; he is not sought after by those who would give or take in marriage, for they would say that a man who is a gambler cannot afford to keep a wife.

Six, young householder, are the perils of the habit of idleness: he says, it is too cold, and does no work. He says, it is too hot and does no work; he says, it is too early... too late, and does no work. He says, I am too hungry and does no work... too full, and does no work. And while all that he should do remains undone, new wealth he does not get, and such wealth as he has dwindles away."

Thus sake the Exalted One. And when the Blessed One had thus spoken, the Master spake again:

"Some friends are bottle-comrades; some are they
Who [to your face] dear friend! dear friend! will say.
Who proves a comrade in your hour of need,
Him may ye rightly call a friend indeed.

Sleeping when sun has risen, adultery,
Entanglement in strife, and doing harm,
Friendship with wicked men, hardness of heart
These causes six to ruin bring a man.
Is he of evil men comrade and friend,
Doth he in evil ways order his life,
Both from this world and from the world to come
To woeful ruin such a man doth fall.

Dicing and women, drink, the dance and song,
Sleeping by day, prowling around at night,
Friendship with wicked men, hardness of heart:

These causes six to ruin bring a man.

Playing with dice, drinking strong drink, he goes
To women dear as life to other men,
Following the baser, not th'enlightened minds,
He wanes as in the darker half the moon.

The tippler of strong drink, poor destitute,
Athirst while drinking, haunter of the bar,
As stone in water so he sinks in debt;
Swift will he make his folk without a name.

One who by habit in the day doth sleep,
Who looks upon the night as time to arise,
One who is ever wanton, filled with wine,
He is not fit to lead a household life.

Too cold! too hot! too late! such is the cry.
And so past men who shake off work that waits
The opportunities for good pass by.
But he who reckons cold and heat as less
Than straws, doing his duties as a man,
He no wise falls away from happiness."

"Four, O young householder, are they who should be reckoned as foes in the likeness of friends: to wit, a rapacious person, the man of words not deeds, the flatterer, the fellow-waster.

Of these the first is on four grounds to be reckoned as a foe in the likeness of a friend: he is rapacious; he gives little and asks much; he does his duty out of fear; he pursues his own interests.

On four grounds the man of words, not deeds, is to be reckoned as a foe in the likeness of a friend: he makes friendly profession in the likeness of a friend; he makes friendly profession as regards the past; he makes friendly profession as regards the future; he tries to gain your favour by empty sayings; when the opportunity for service has arisen he avows his disability.

On four grounds the flatterer is to be reckoned as a foe in the likeness of a friend: he both consents to do wrong, and dissents from doing right; he praises you to your face; he speaks ill of you to others.

On four grounds the fellow-waster companion is to be reckoned as a foe in the likeness of a friend: he is your companion when you indulge in strong drink; he is your companion when you frequent the streets at untimely hours; he is your companion when you haunt shows and fairs; he is your companion when you are infatuated with gambling."

Thus spake the Exalted One. And when the Blessed One had thus spoken, the Master sake yet again:

> "The friend who's ever seeking what to take,
> The friend whose words are other than his deeds,
> The friend who flatters, pleasing you withal.
> The boon companion down the current ways–
> These four are foes. Thus having recognized,
> Let the wise man avoid them from afar
> As they were path of peril and of dread."

"Four, O young householder, are the friends who should be reckoned as sound at heart–the helper; the friend who is the same in happiness and adversity; the friend of good council; the friend who sympathises.

On four grounds the friend who is a helper is to be reckoned as sound at heart: he guards you when you are off your guard, he guards your property when you are off your guard; he is a refuge to you when you are afraid; when you have tasks to perform he provides a double supply [of what you may need].

On four grounds the friend who is the same in happiness and adversity is to be reckoned as sound of heart: he tells you his secrets; he keeps secret your secrets; in your troubles he does not forsake you; he lays down even his life for your sake.

On four grounds the friend who declares what you need to do is. . . sound at heart: he restrains you from doing wrong; he enjoins you to [do what is] right; he informs you of what you had not heard before; he reveals to you the way to heaven.

On four grounds the friend who sympathises is to be reckoned as sound at heart: he does not rejoice over your misfortunes; he rejoices over your prosperity; he restrains anyone who is speaking ill of you; he commends anyone who is praising you."

Thus sake the Exalted One. And when the Blessed One had thus spoken, the Master sake yet again:

> "The friend who is a helpmate, and the friend
> Of bright days and of dark, and he who shows
> What't is you need, and he who throbs for you
> With sympathy: these four the wise should know
> As friends, and should devote himself to them
> As mother to her own, her bosom's child.
> Whoso is virtuous and intelligent,
> Shines like a fire that blazes [on the hill].
> To him amassing wealth, like roving bee
> Its honey gathering [and hurting naught],
> Riches mount up as ant-heap growing high.
> When the good layman wealth has so amassed
> Able is he to benefit his clan.
> In portions four let him divide that wealth.
> So binds he to himself life's friendly things.
> One portion let him spend and taste the fruit.
> His business to conduct let him take two.
> And portion four let him reserve and hoard;
> So there'll be wherewithal in times of need."

"And how, O young householder, does the ariyan disciple protect the six quarters? The following should be looked upon as the six quarters–parents as the east, teachers as the south, wife and children as the west, friends and companions as the north, servants and work people as the nadir, religious teachers and brahmins as the zenith.

"In five ways a child should minister to his parents as the eastern quarter. Once supported by them I will now be their support; I will perform duties incumbent on them; I will keep up the lineage and tradition of my family; I will make myself worthy of my heritage.

In five ways parents thus ministered to, as the eastern quarter, by their child, show their love for him: they restrain him from vice, they exhort him to virtue, they train him to a profession, they contract a suitable marriage for him, and in due time they hand over his inheritance.

Thus is this eastern quarter protected by him and made safe and secure.

In five ways should pupils minister to their teachers as the southern quarter: by rising (from their seat, in salutation) by waiting upon them, by eagerness to learn, by personal service, and by attention when receiving their teaching.

And in five ways do teachers, thus ministered to as the southern quarter by their pupils, love their pupil: they train him in that wherein he has been well trained; they make him hold fast that which is well held; they thoroughly instruct him in the lore of every art; they speak well of him among his friends and companions. They provide for his safety in every quarter.

Thus is this quarter protected by him and made safe and secure.

In five ways should a wife as western quarter be ministered to by her husband: by respect, by courtesy, by faithfulness, by handing over authority to her, by providing her with adornment.

In these five ways does the wife, ministered to by her husband as the western quarter, love him: her duties are well performed, by hospitality to the kin of both, by faithfulness, by watching over the goods he brings, and by skill and industry in discharging all her business.

Thus is this western quarter protected by him and made safe and secure.

In five ways should a clansman minister to his friends and familiars as the northern quarter: by generosity, courtesy and benevolence, by treating them as he treats himself, and by being as good as his word.

In these five ways thus ministered to as the northern quarter, his friends and familiars love him: they protect him when he is off his guard, and on such occasions guard his property; they become a refuge in danger, they do not forsake him in his troubles, and they show consideration for his family.

Thus is the northern quarter by him protected and made safe and secure.

In five ways does an ariyan master minister to his servants and employees as the nadir: by assigning them work according to their strength; by supplying them with food and wages; by tending them in sickness; by sharing with them unusual delicacies; by granting leave at times.

In these ways ministered to by their master, servants and employees love their master in five ways: they rise before him, they lie down to rest after him; they are content with what is given to them; they do their work well; and they carry about his praise and good fame.

Thus is the nadir by him protected and made safe and secure.

In five ways should the clansman minister to recluses and brahmins as the zenith: by affection in act speech and mind; by keeping open house to them, by supplying their temporal needs.

Thus ministered to as the zenith, recluses and brahmins show their love for the clansman in six ways: they restrain him from evil, they exhort him to good, they love him with kindly thoughts; they teach him what he had not heard, they correct and purify what he has heard, they reveal to him the way to heaven.

"Thus by him is the zenith protected and made safe and secure."

Thus sake the Exalted One. And when the Blessed One had so spoken, the Master said yet further:

"Mother and father are the Eastern view,
And teachers are the quarters of the South.
And wife and children are the Western view,
And friends and kin the quarter to the North;
Servants and working folk the nadir are,
And overhead the brahmin and recluse.
These quarters should be worshipped by the man
Who fitly ranks as houseman in his clan.

He that is wise, expert in virtue's ways,
Gentle and in this worship eloquent,
Humble and docile, he may honour win.
Active in rising, foe to laziness,
Unshaken in adversities, his life
Flawless, sagacious, he may honour win.
If he have winning ways, and maketh friends,
Makes welcome with kind words and generous heart,
And can give sage councils and advice,
And guide his fellows, he may honour win.

The giving hand, the kindly speech, the life
Of service, impartiality to one
As to another, as the case demands
These be the things that make the world go round
As linchpin serves the rolling of the car.
And if these things be not, no mother reaps
The honour and respect her child should pay,
Nor doth the father win them through the child.
And since the wise rightly appraise these things,

They win to eminence and earn men's praise."

When the Exalted One had thus spoken, Sigāla the young householder said this: Beautiful, lord, beautiful! As if one should set up again that which had been overthrown, or reveal that which had been hidden, or should disclose the road to one that was astray, or should carry a lamp into darkness, saying They that have eyes will see! Even so hath the Truth been manifested by the Exalted One in many ways. And I, even I, do go to him as my refuge, and to the Truth and to the Order. May the Exalted One receive me as his lay-disciple, as one has taken his refuge in him from this day forth as long as life endures."

Udāna: (VIII, viii)

Thus have I heard: On a certain occasion the Exalted One was staying near Sāvatthī in East Park, at the storeyed house of Migāra's mother.

Now at that time the dear and lovely grand-daughter of Visākhā, Migāra's mother, had died. So Visākhā, Migāra's mother, with clothes and hair still wet (from washing) came at an unseasonable hour to see the Exalted One, and on coming to him, saluted him and sat down at one side. As she sat thus the Exalted One said this to Visākhā, Migāra's mother:

"Why, Visākhā! How is it that you come here with clothes and hair still wet at an unseasonable hour?"

"O, sir, my dear and lovely grand-daughter is dead! That is why I come here with hair and clothes still wet at an unseasonable hour."

"Visākhā, would you like to have as many sons and grandsons as there are men in Sāvatthī?"

"Yes, sir, I would indeed!"

"But how many men do you suppose die daily in Sāvatthī?'

'Ten, sir, or maybe nine, or eight. Maybe seven, six, five or four, three, two; maybe one a day dies in Sāvatthī, sir. Sāvatthī is never free from men dying, sir."

"What think you, Visākhā? In such case would you ever be without wet hair and clothes?"

"Surely not, sir! Enough for me, sir, of so many sons and grandsons!"

"Visākhā, whoso have a hundred things beloved, they have a hundred sorrows. Whoso have ninety, eighty... thirty, twenty things beloved...

whoso have ten... whoso have but one thing beloved, have but one sorrow. Sorrowless are they and passionless. Serene are they, I declare."

> "All griefs or lamentations whatso'er
> And divers forms of sorrow in the world,
> Because of what is dear do these become.
> Thing dear not being, these do not become.
> Happy are they therefore and free from grief
> To whom is naught at all dear in the world.
> Wherefore aspiring for the griefless, sorrowless,
> Make thou in all the world naught dear to thee."

Itivuttaka: (III, IV,vii)

"Monks, these three unprofitable ways of thinking cause blindness, loss of sight, ignorance, put an end to insight, are associated with trouble and conduce not to nibbāna. What three ways of thinking?

Thinking about lust... about ill-will... about harming... causes blindness, loss of sight... conduces not to nibbāna. These are the three.

Monks, these three profitable ways of thinking cause not blindness, but cause sight, knowledge, increase insight, are on the side of freedom from trouble and conduce to nibbāna. What three?

Thinking about renunciation... goodwill... harmlessness conduce to nibbāna. These three profitable ways of thinking... conduce to nibbāna."

Three profitable ways of thought should one pursue,
And three unprofitable ways should put away,
He surely doth control a train of thought sustained,
As a rain-shower lays accumulated dust,
He surely with a mind that lays its thought to rest,
In this same life (on earth) hath reached
the place of peace.

12
Pāli glossary

Editors note

This Pāli glossary is generic and not specifically made for this book. Although there are Pāli words in the text that may not be in this glossary, they are defined as they are introduced.

abhiñña supernormal power

adhimokkha determination (a cetasika)

adhipati paccaya predominance condition

adosa non-aversion or kindness(a cetasika)

ahetuka rootless (citta)

ahetuka diṭṭhi the wrong view of no cause for what arises

ahirika shamelessness(a cetasika)

ākāsānañcāyatana sphere of boundless space, the subject of the first arūpa jhāna-citta

ākiñcaññāyatana sphere of nothingness, the subject of the third arūpal jhāna-citta

akusala unwholesome

alobha non-attachment or generosity (a cetasika)

amoha understanding(a cetasika)

anāgāmī non-returner, the noble person who has realised the third stage of enlightenment

anantara paccaya proximity condition

anattā non-self

anicca impermanent

anottappa recklessness or disregard of unwholesomeness(a cetasika)

anuloma adaptation (citta) arising before jhāna or before enlightenment

anumodhana asking beings to rejoice in the good deeds which one has done and so benefit themselves

anupādisesa nibbāna final nibbāna, khandha parinibbāna at the death of an arahat

anusaya latent tendency

āpo dhātu element of water

appaṇā (samādhi) absorption (concentration)

arahat noble person who has attained the fourth stage of enlightenment

ārammaṇa the object of consciousness

ariyan noble, the person who has attained enlightenment

arūpa-brahma-bhūmi plane of existence of immaterial beings. Birth as a result of attaining arūpa jhāna

arūpavacara belonging to the immaterial plane of consciousness, arūpa-jhāna-citta

arūpa-jhāna immaterial absorption

asankhārika strong (cittas) spontaneously arisen, not induced by others

āsava cankers, influxes of intoxicants, group of defilements

asobhana not beautiful, not accompanied by beautiful roots

asūbha foul

asura demon, being of one of the unhappy planes of existence

ātāpī heedful, with awareness

atīta bhavaṅga past life-continuum, arising and falling away shortly before a process of citta experiencing an object through one of the sense-doors starts

āvajjana adverting of consciousness to the object which has impinged on one of the six doors

avijjā ignorance

avyākata dhammas (realities) which are not kusala or akusala

ayoniso manasikāra unwise attention to an object

āyūhana kamma at birth which brings results during a lifetime

bhāvanā mental development, the development of calm, samatha, and the development of insight, vipassanā

bhāvanā-māya-paññā understanding based on mental development

bhavaṅga citta life-continuum citta which does not arise within a process but in between processes

bhavaṅga calana vibrating bhavaṅga, arising shortly before a sense-cognition process starts

bhavaṅgupaccheda arrest bhavaṅga, last bhavaṅga-citta before a process starts The bhavaṅgupaccheda which arises before a mind-door process is the mind-door of that process

bhikkhu monk

bhikkhunī nun

bhūmi plane of existence

brahma-vihāra one of the four "divine abidings". which are loving kindness, compassion, sympathetic joy and equanimity

cakkhu eye

cakkhu-dvāra eye-door

cakkhuppasāda rūpa eye-sense

cakkhuviññāṇa seeing-consciousness

cetanā intention or volition (a cetasika)

cetasika mental factor arising with consciousness

chanda interest (a cetasika)

citta consciousness, the chief reality which experiences an object

citta-kammaññatā wieldiness of citta (a cetasika)

citta-lahutā lightness of citta (a cetasika)

citta-mudutā pliancy of citta (a cetasika)

citta-passaddhi tranquility of citta (a cetasika)

citta-pāguññatā proficiency of citta (a cetasika)

citta-ujukatā uprightness of citta (a cetasika)

cuti-citta death consciousness

dāna generosity, giving

dassana kicca function of seeing

dhamma reality, the natural law, the Teaching of The Buddha

dhammārammaṇa any object which can only be experienced through the mind-door

dhātu element, any reality

diṭṭhi wrong view

diṭṭhigata sampayutta accompanied by wrong view

domanassa unpleasant feeling

dosa aversion or ill-will (a cetasika)

dosa-mūla-citta citta rooted in aversion

dukkha vedanā painful feeling or unpleasant feeling

dvāra doorway through which an object is experienced, the five sense-doors or the mind-door

dvi-pañca-viññāṇa the five pairs of sense-cognitions, which are seeing, hearing, smelling, tasting and bodily experience

ekaggatā cetasika one-pointedness which makes citta focus on one object

ghāṇa-dhātu nose element

ghāṇappasāda rūpa nose-sense

ghandha odour

gantha bond, a group of defilements

ghāyana kicca function of smelling

gotrabhū change of lineage citta before jhāna or enlightenment is attained

hadaya-vatthu heart-base

hasituppāda citta smiling-consciousness of the arahat

hetu root

hiri moral shame (a cetasika)

indriya faculty, leader

issā jealousy, envy (a cetasika)

jāti birth, class (of cittas)

javana impulsion (function of cittas) which "run through"the object

jhāna absorption, burning, developed in samatha or vipassanā

jhāyati it burns

jivhā tongue

jivhāppasāda rūpa tongue base

jīvitindriya life-faculty (a cetasika or a rūpa)

kalyāṇa mitta good friend

kāma bhūmi sensuous plane of existence

kāmāvacara citta sense-sphere cconsciousness

kamma intention or volition; deed motivated by volition

kammaṭṭhāna object of samatha bhāvanā

kamma-patha course of action, which is wholesome or unwholesome

kappa a world cycle; an aeon

karuṇā compassion (a cetasika)

kasiṇa disk, as meditation subject in the development of calm, samatha

kāya collection, body of rūpas or mental body, the cetasikas

kāya-dhātu body-sense element

kāya-kammaññatā wieldiness of cetasikas (a cetasika)

kāya-lahutā lightness of cetasikas (a cetasika)

kāya-mudutā pliancy of cetasikas (a cetasika)

kāya-pāguññatā proficiency of cetasikas (a cetasika)

kāya-passaddhi tranquility of cetasikas (a cetasika)

kāyappasāda rūpa body-sense

kāya-ujukatā uprightness of cetasikas (a cetasika)

kāyaviññāṇa body consciousness

kāya-viññatti bodily intimation (a rūpa)

khandha one of a group, any conditioned reality, i.e. any rūpa, vedanā, saññā, saṇkhāra or viññāna

kiriya citta inoperative citta which is not kusala, akusala or vipāka

kukkucca regret, worry (a cetasika)

lakkhaṇa characteristic

lobha attachment (a cetasika)

lobha-mūla-citta citta rooted in attachment

lokiya citta mundane citta

lokuttara citta supramundane citta which experiences nibbāna

lokuttara dhamma nibbāna and a citta or cetasika which experiences nibbāna

macchariya stinginess (a cetasika)

magga path, Eightfold Path

magga-citta path-consciousness, lokuttara citta which experiences nibbāna and eradicates defilements

mahā-bhūta rūpa the rūpa which is one of the four great elements of earth or solidity, water or cohesion, fire or temperature and wind or motion

māna conceit (a cetasika)

manasikāra attention (a cetasika)

mano consciousness, citta

mano-dhātu mind-element. The five-sense-door adverting-consciousness and the two types of receiving consciousness

mano-dvārāvajjana-citta mind-door adverting-consciousness

mano-dvāra-vīthi-citta citta arising in a mind-door process

manoviññāṇa dhātu mind-consciousness element. All cittas other than the sense-cognitions (seeing, etc.) and mind-element cittas

mettā loving kindness

middha torpor (a cetasika)

moha ignorance (a cetasika)

moha-mūla-citta citta rooted in ignorance

muditā sympathetic joy (a cetasika)

mūla root

nāma any reality which can experience an object

natthika diṭṭhi wrong view that there is no result of kamma

n'eva-saññā-n'āsaññāyatana sphere of neither perception nor non-perception, the object of the fourth immaterial jhāna

nibbāna the unconditioned reality which is freedom from dukkha

nimitta mental image or sign

nirodha-samāpatti attainment of cessation of consciousness

nīvaraṇa hindrance, defilement

ñāṇa wisdom, understanding

oja nutriment (a rūpa)

oḷārika rūpa gross rūpa. Any sense-object or sense-base

ottappa blameless (a cetasika)

paccaya condition

pakatūpanissaya paccaya natural decisive support condition

Pāli language of the Buddhist Pāli Canon

pāṇātipāta killing

pañcadvārāvajjana citta five sense-door adverting-consciousness

(dvi-)pañca-viññāṇa citta sense-consciousness (seeing, etc.). There are five pairs

paññā wisdom or understanding

paññatti concept which makes known

paramattha dhamma absolute, ultimate reality

pāramī perfection, 10 pāramī

parikamma citta preparatory consciousness

pariyatti intellectual right understanding of reality

pasāda-rūpa sense-base (eye-sense, ear-sense, nose-sense, tongue-sense, body-sense)

paṭibhāga nimitta counterpart image acquired in the development of calm, samatha

paṭicca samuppāda dependent origination

paṭigha aversion, ill-will, dosa (a cetasika)

Pātimokkha rules for monks

paṭipatti direct understanding of reality, literally reaching the particular (object)

paṭisandhi citta rebirth consciousness

phala-citta fruit-consciousness which experiences nibbāna as a result of magga citta

phassa contact (a cetasika)

phoṭṭhabbārammaṇa tangible object, experienced through body sense (hardness/softness, heat/cold or motion)

phusana kicca function of experiencing tangible object

pīti joy (a cetasika)

puthujjana worldling, ordinary person

rasa taste

rūpa physical reality which cannot experience anything

rūpa-bhūmi plane of beings where birth was the result of rūpa-jhāna, fine-material jhāna

rūpa-brahma-bhūmi fine material plane of existence

rūpa-jhāna fine material absorption

rūpa-khandha any rūpa, one of group of physical phenomena

rūpāvacara citta consciousness of the fine-material sphere, rūpa-jhāna-citta

sabhāva nature, characteristic of reality

sadda sound

saddhā faith or confidence in wholesomeness

sahetuka accompanied by roots

sakadāgāmī once-returner, noble person who has attained the second stage of enlightenment

samādhi concentration or one-pointedness

samatha

sammā-diṭṭhi right understanding

sammā-sati right awareness

sampaṭicchana-citta receiving-consciousness

sampayutta associated with

saṃsāra cycle of births and deaths

saṅkhāra dhamma conditioned reality

saṅkhārakkhandha all cetasikas other than vedanā (feeling) and saññā (memory)

saññā perception or memory

santīraṇa-citta investigating-consciousness

sasaṅkhārika induced by oneself or someone else, weak (citta)

sassatavāda diṭṭhi eternalist view

sati awareness (a cetasika)

sati-sampajanna mindfulness and clear comprehension of purpose

satipaṭṭhāna awareness of a reality. It can be the cetasika sati or the object of mindfulness

sa-upādi-sesa nibbāna arahatship with the khandhas or "groups of existing" remaining

sīla morality, behaviour of cittas

sīlabbatupādāna wrong practice which is clinging to certain rules (rites and rituals)

sobhana beautiful, accompanied by beautiful roots

somanassa pleasant feeling

sota-dhātu element of ear

sota-dvāra-vīthi ear-door process

sotāpanna noble person who has attained the first stage of enlightenment

sota viññāṇa hearing-consciousness

sukha-vedanā pleasant feeling

suttas sayings of the Buddha

tadālambana/tadārammaṇa retention or registering, last citta of a complete process

Tathāgata "Thus-gone", The Buddha

tatramajjhattatā equanimity or even-mindedness (a cetasika)

tejo dhātu element of fire or heat

thīna sloth (a cetasika)

uddhacca restlessness (a cetasika)

upacāra access or proximity (concentration)

upādā rūpa derived rūpa, any rūpa other than the four great elements

upādāna clinging

upādānakkhandha any khandha which is the object of clinging

upekkhā indifferent feeling or equanimity

vacī-viññatti speech intimation (a rūpa)

vatthu base, physical base of citta

vāyo dhātu element of wind or motion

vedanā feeling (a cetasika)

vicāra sustained thought

vicikicchā doubt (a cetasika)

vinaya discipline for monks

viññāṇa consciousness

viññāṇa khandha aggregate of consciousness, any citta

viññāṇañcāyatana sphere of boundless consciousness, subject for the second stage of immaterial jhāna

vipāka citta (and cetasikas) which are the result of kamma

vipallāsa perversion

vipassanā insight, wisdom which sees realities as they are

vippayutta unaccompanied by

viriya energy, effort, patience (a cetasika)

vitakka striking, directs the citta to the object (a cetasika)

vīthicitta citta arising in a process

vīthi-vimutti-citta process freed citta, citta which does not arise within a process

voṭṭhapana determining consciousness

vyāpāda ill-will

yoniso manasikāra wise attention

13

Books by Nina van Gorkom

- *The Buddha's Path.* An Introduction to the doctrine of Theravada Buddhism for those who have no previous knowledge. The four noble Truths - suffering - the origin of suffering - the cessation of suffering - and the way leading to the end of suffering - are explained as a philosophy and a practical guide which can be followed in today's world.

- *Buddhism in Daily Life.* A general introduction to the main ideas of Theravāda Buddhism.The purpose of this book is to help the reader gain insight into the Buddhist scriptures and the way in which the teachings can be used to benefit both ourselves and others in everyday life.

- *Abhidhamma in Daily Life* is an exposition of absolute realities in detail. Abhidhamma means higher doctrine and the book's purpose is to encourage the right application of Buddhism in order to eradicate wrong view and eventually all defilements.

- *Cetasikas.* Cetasika means 'belonging to the mind'. It is a mental factor which accompanies consciousness (citta) and experiences an object. There are 52 cetasikas. This book gives an outline of each of these 52 cetasikas and shows the relationship they have with each other.

- *The Buddhist Teaching on Physical Phenomena.* A general introduction to physical phenomena and the way they are related to each other and to mental phenomena. The purpose of this book is to show that the study of both mental phenomena and physical phenomena is indispensable for the development of the Eightfold Path.

- *The Conditionality of Life.* This book is an introduction to the seventh book of the Abhidhamma, that deals with the conditionality of life. It explains the deep underlying motives for all actions through body, speech and mind and shows that these are dependent on conditions and cannot be controlled by a 'self'. This book is suitable for those who have already made a study of the Buddha's teachings.

- *Letters on Vipassanā.* This book consists of a compilation of letters on the Dhamma to Sarah Abbott, Alan Weller, Robert Kirkpatrick and other friends. The materials used are tapes of Khun Sujin's lectures and conversations with her on the development of right understanding. She encourages people to develop the understanding of the present moment, since that is the way to the ultimate goal, namely, the eradication of the clinging to the concept of self and of all other defilements.

- *A Survey of Paramattha Dhammas* by Sujin Boriharnwanaket, translated by Nina van Gorkom. A Survey of Paramattha Dhammas is a guide to the development of the Buddha's path of wisdom, covering all aspects of human life and human behaviour, good and bad. This study explains that right understanding is indispensable for mental development, the development of calm as well as the development of insight.

- *The Perfections Leading to Enlightenment* by Sujin Boriharnwanaket, translated by Nina van Gorkom. The Perfections is a study of the ten good qualities: generosity, morality, renunciation, wisdom, energy, patience, truthfulness, determination, loving-kindness, and equanimity.

- *An Introduction to the Buddhist scriptures* with the aim to encourage the reader to study the texts themselves. In that way they can verify that the Buddha's words were directed to the practice of what he taught, in particular to the development of right understanding of all phenomena of life.

- *Understanding Realities Now: Nina's Travelogues.* Compilation of articles discussing the development of insight, the understanding of the present moment in daily life. It contains over 60 quotes from the original scriptures and commentaries.

- *Buddhism: Learning to understand life.* The purpose of this book is to help the reader gain insight into how Buddhism works to understand life. It is not mere theory, but it is to be applied right now, at this moment. The Buddha taught that all mental phenomena and physical phenomena which naturally appear in our daily life can be objects of mindfulness and right understanding. (Also available on Amazon Kindle).

- *Understanding Life Now*, authors Sarah Procter Abbott and Nina van Gorkom. Published 26th January 2022. This book consists of 276 Jottings taken from Zoom discussions during the Covid-19 pandemic. They are all about the truth of life at the present moment as taught by the Buddha. They are for anyone with an interest in learning more about what is most precious in life: the understanding of what is real now as opposed to what we assume to be real.

- *The World in the Buddhist Sense*, author Nina van Gorkom. Published July 1st 2022. The purpose of this book is to show that the Buddha's Path to true understanding has to be developed in daily life. It explains the pitfalls one will come across while developing this path and the way to overcome them. The book is composed of letters written in answer to questions about the practice. It is suitable for any person interested to know how Buddhism understands the world.

www.ingramcontent.com/pod-product-compliance
Lightning Source LLC
Chambersburg PA
CBHW011758040426
42446CB00019B/3460
* 9 7 8 1 8 9 7 6 3 3 5 2 6 *